THE 2 INGREDIENT COOK BOOK

The EASY way to make delicious meals FAST!

ADELINE ROSEMIRE

MERIDIAN PUBLISHING, INC.
SAN JOSE, CALIFORNIA

Library of Congress Cataloging-in-Publication Data

Rosemire, Adeline.
  The 2-ingredient cookbook.

  Includes index.
  1. Quick and easy cookery. I. Title.
TX833.5.R67 1996   95-37458
641.5'55--dc20

Published by Meridian Publishing, Inc.
2431 Tulip Road, San Jose, CA 95128

Every effort has been made to avoid using previously copyrighted
recipes in this book. If, in spite of our best efforts, such a recipe
should appear in this book, it is without our knowledge and is wholly
unintentional.

ISBN 0-9640044-8-8

Printed and bound in the United States of America.

Acknowledgments

Special thanks to my husband, recipe tester, and editor.

Thanks also to the generous friends, family members and companies who contributed their recipes and support.

Dedication

This book is dedicated to my aunt, Evelyn Silveira, who was one of the finest cooks and persons I've ever known.

Contents

Introduction

I have written this book as much for myself as for everyone who reads it. It's a revolutionary book written to help us with our revolutionary lifestyles. Few people have the luxury of time that it takes to cook lavish meals on a daily basis, or even for special occasions. Other people simply don't have the interest in cooking; they would rather spend time pursuing interests that they find more fun, more fulfilling, more lucrative, or more relaxing.

I'll be the first to admit that there are zillions of cookbooks available, many with titles that include the words 'quick' and 'easy'... words that you can't trust anymore. In some cases, 'quick' means throwing together 18 ingredients, and 'easy' means you don't have to grow your own corn—it's all relative.

This book will save you time at the grocery store (think express line), as well as in the kitchen. Just picture yourself in and out of the grocery store in 10 minutes, picking up 8 ingredients, and having everything you need for a suitably impressive 4-course dinner party. Read that again: 10 minutes + 8 ingredients = a terrific dinner at home.

The 2-Ingredient Cookbook is perfect for working people, single parents, college students, travelers or anyone short on time. It can help you prepare food *almost* as quickly as purchasing fast food, and it will almost certainly be better for you. It's also a great way to introduce children, who are long on time but short on attention spans, to the world of cooking. Tell them each recipe is a short story with a happy ending.

I hope you enjoy using *The 2-Ingredient Cookbook* as much as I enjoyed researching and developing it.

A note about the 2-ingredient philosophy

In the 2-ingredient world, the assumption is made that you have certain culinary essentials already relaxing in your kitchen. These essentials include *small amounts* of salt and pepper; basic spices such as nutmeg and cumin; oil and/or non-stick vegetable spray; butter; water; milk; sugar and flour—none of which I counted as 'third ingredients'. Oh, and ice for some of the beverage recipes. This 'fudge factor' allowed me to add several great recipes to this book—recipes that aren't strictly 2-ingredient efforts, but are too good not to share with you.

In this book, 2 ingredients means 2 items. Consider the ambiguity of counting ingredients: Many people would count catsup as 1 ingredient in a recipe, yet catsup is comprised of *several* ingredients. If you find yourself inclined to point out that some recipes contain more than two ingredients, I would like to ask you for a little cooking mercy. Just take a deep breath, relax, and enjoy the time you've saved by using these recipes.

One final note: I have listed optional ingredients in several recipes. Whether or not you use these optional ingredients, I want you to know that the dishes will be delicious. Each recipe in the book was selected for its flavor, speed of assembly, and ease of preparation. In other words, food that is tasty, yet fast, fast, fast.

Breakfast/Brunch

❧ Hearty Fare ❦

Baked-Ahead Honey Bacon
   ½ pound bacon, thick cut
   3 tablespoons honey

Line a broiling pan or 10x15-inch baking pan with foil. Place bacon side by side on foil (you may overlap strips if necessary). Bake at 350 degrees for 10-15 minutes until the edges turn brown. Remove from oven and drain the excess fat. Drizzle honey over bacon. Return to oven and bake 15-20 additional minutes, until well browned. Let stand for 5 minutes to cool. Serves 4.

Note: Any type of bacon can be cooked, put into a sealed bag, and frozen until you are ready to astonish your breakfast guests with *instant* bacon. Just heat the bacon in an oven, or microwave for 1 minute on medium-high.

Two-Ingredient Spreads and Toppings for Bagels

- **Mix ½ cup peanut butter and 1 3-ounce package cream cheese, room temperature. Add 2 teaspoons honey, if desired. Spread on toasted bagel halves.**

- **Top a toasted, split bagel with cheddar cheese and ham strips.**

- **Top a toasted, split bagel with Monterey jack cheese and turkey slices.**

Two-Ingredient Fillings For Flour Tortillas
- scrambled eggs and salsa
- peanut butter and honey
- peanut butter and banana slices
- low-fat ricotta or cream cheese and sliced berries

Warm tortillas in a 400-degree oven for 2 minutes, or place tortillas between 2 damp paper towels and microwave for 1 minute on high. Spoon filling into warmed tortillas.

Omelet

> 3 eggs
>
> 2 tablespoons milk
>
> 1 tablespoon butter, optional

Beat eggs and milk in a small bowl. Pour the mixture into a medium size skillet sprayed with non-stick vegetable spray or butter. Cook on medium-low heat until the eggs on bottom begin to set; push aside or lift cooked egg to let liquid egg flow to the pan bottom. Repeat until eggs are set, but still creamy-looking on top, about 7 minutes.

Variations: Sauté or steam a few vegetables and serve them wrapped (camouflaged) in the omelet. Asparagus, broccoli, cauliflower, potatoes, and spinach are especially good. (This is a great way to get rid of leftovers.) Cooked sausage, sautéed mushrooms, and chopped scallions are also terrific. Or heat a 10-ounce favorite package of frozen vegetables in cheese sauce and pour it over the cooked eggs before folding the omelet in half.

Sunday Morning Scrambled Eggs

4 eggs

¼ cup Pace Picante Sauce

Mix eggs and salsa in a small bowl. Spray skillet with vegetable spray. Heat skillet over medium flame for 1 minute. Add 1 tablespoon butter or olive oil to skillet, if desired, and heat for 1 minute. Pour mixture into skillet and stir occasionally, until eggs are set, about 4 minutes. Serves 2.

Muffin Tin Breakfast

1 8-ounce box Jiffy corn muffin mix

1 15-ounce can corned beef hash

Preheat oven to 400 degrees. Grease or spray a muffin tin with non-stick spray. Prepare corn muffin mix according to directions (you might need 1 egg or milk). Fill half of the muffin tin openings with the muffin mixture. Fill the other half with corned beef hash. Bake for 20 minutes, or according to the directions on the muffin mix box. Serves 4.

Variation: Indent each mound of hash and drop an egg into it before baking.

Just-Add-Water Pancakes

1 7-ounce container Bisquick Shake 'n Pour Buttermilk Pancake Mix (found next to flour and baking ingredients at the grocer)

1 tablespoon oil

Follow the directions on the container. (This involves adding water and shaking the container.) Cook pancakes in large skillet with 1 tablespoon heated oil. Serve with butter and syrup. Makes 8-10 pancakes.

Oven Pancakes and Sausage

1 7-ounce container Bisquick Shake 'n Pour Buttermilk Pancake Mix

1 8-ounce box Brown 'n Serve frozen sausages

Preheat oven to 450 degrees. Follow directions on the pancake mix container for making 8 pancakes (this amounts to adding water and shaking the container). Butter or grease a 13x9x2-inch baking pan. Pour pancake mixture into pan and arrange sausage links on top. Bake for 12-15 minutes. Cut into 6 squares. Serve with hot syrup or butter. Serves 6.

Sizzling Zucchini

4 slices bacon, cubed

2 cups zucchini, cubed (about 2 zucchini)

Cube bacon and zucchini. Fry bacon in a large skillet over medium heat. After bacon is crisp, remove most of the drippings. Add zucchini, and salt and pepper, if desired. Cover and cook over low heat for 15-20 minutes, stirring once. Serves 2.

❧ Croissants ❧

Ham and Cheese Croissant Filling

8 ounces cooked ham, sliced thin

8 ounces brie cheese, cut in 8 thin wedges or slices

Preheat oven to 325 degrees. Place 4 croissants, each with 2 slits cut from top almost through bottom, on a foil-lined baking sheet. Tuck a ham slice and cheese wedge into each slit. Bake for about 9 minutes until cheese starts to melt. (If using frozen croissants, prepare according to package directions, making slits in croissants while still frozen. After baking, remove from oven, add filling and return to oven for 2-3 minutes.) Makes 4 servings.

Orange-Pecan Croissant Filling

8 teaspoons orange marmalade

¼ cup chopped pecans

Preheat oven to 325 degrees. Slit 4 croissants 1 inch deep along the
top. Spread 1 teaspoon marmalade in each croissant slit. Fill with 1
tablespoon pecans, then another teaspoon marmalade. Bake on baking
sheet for 10 minutes. (If using frozen croissants, prepare according to
package directions, making slit in croissants while still frozen. After
baking, remove from oven, add filling and return to oven for 2-3
minutes.) Serve hot. Makes 4.

Cherry-Cream Croissant Filling

1½ cups vanilla ice cream

1 15-ounce can cherry pie filling

Preheat oven to 325 degrees. Slit 4 croissants 1 inch deep along the
top. Place crumpled foil in each slit to hold croissant open. Bake 10
minutes until crisp. (If using frozen croissants, prepare according to
package directions, making slit in croissants while still frozen. After
baking, remove from oven, insert foil and return to oven for 2-3
minutes.) Cool completely, 15-20 minutes. Remove foil; place
croissants on serving plates. Fill each slit with ice cream; spoon
cherry filling over ice cream. Makes 4 servings. Great for those
occasions with red and white themes; e.g., Valentine's Day,
Christmas, and 4th of July (if you throw in blueberries).

❧ Fruit ❧

Golden Grapefruit

1 grapefruit, halved and sectioned

4 teaspoons brown sugar

Sprinkle 2 teaspoons brown sugar on each grapefruit half. Broil 1-2
minutes or bake for 5-7 minutes in a 350-degree oven. Serves 2.

Cream Sauce for Fruit

> **1 8-ounce container vanilla yogurt**
>
> **3 tablespoons brown sugar**

Combine yogurt and brown sugar in a small bowl. Let stand 5 minutes to let brown sugar melt into yogurt. Stir and pour sauce over fruit or offer as a fruit dip. Makes 1 cup.

Strawberry Sauce for Fruit

> **2 cups fresh strawberries, hulled and rinsed, or 1 10-ounce container frozen strawberries, thawed**
>
> **1 tablespoon sugar**

In a blender or food processor, whirl hulled strawberries and sugar until smooth. If making ahead, cover strawberry sauce and chill up to 2 days. Serve over pineapple, kiwi fruit, papaya, bananas, or your favorite fruit. Makes 1 cup sauce.

Variation: Add 2 tablespoons orange-flavor liqueur such as Grand Marnier.

❧ Beverages ❦

Orange Sunrise

> **1 cup orange juice**
>
> **1 tablespoon grenadine syrup (found shelved with cocktail mixes, although it's nonalcoholic)**

To each glass of chilled orange juice, add 1 tablespoon of grenadine. The combination creates a lovely sunrise color when mixed, or add grenadine to the orange juice and let it sink to the bottom of the glass; stir to drink. Serves 1.

Knock-You-on-Your-Navel Orange Juice

1 cup orange juice

1 ounce Peachtree Schnapps

½ ounce vodka, optional

To each glass of chilled orange juice, add 1 ounce Peachtree Schnapps, and ½ ounce vodka, if desired. Serves 1.

Hot Schnapps

8 ounces hot chocolate

1 ounce Peppermint Schnapps

To each mug of hot chocolate, add 1 ounce Peppermint Schnapps. Serves 1.

Variation: Top with whipped cream, if desired.

The-Morning-Before Iced Coffee

1 cup leftover morning coffee, frozen into cubes at least 24 hours

fresh-brewed coffee, room temperature

For each serving of iced coffee, place six coffee ice cubes in a tall glass. Pour room-temperature, fresh-brewed coffee over cubes. Serve with cream and powdered sugar, if desired.

Variation: Before brewing, sprinkle ground cinnamon over the grounds, using one teaspoon cinnamon for 10 to 12 cups coffee. Brew, then cool and serve over coffee ice cubes.

The-Morning-After Whipped Coffee

    1 cup hot coffee

    1 teaspoon whipped or heavy cream, or frozen dessert topping (thawed)

    1 tablespoon cognac, optional

To one cup of coffee add 1 tablespoon cognac, if desired. Top with 1 teaspoon whipped or heavy cream. Serves 1.

2

Appetizers/Party Food

❧ Dips ❧

Adobe Dip

1 8-ounce jar spicy bean dip
1 8-ounce container sour cream

Mix ingredients. Serve with tortilla chips. Makes 2 cups.

Adobe Dip Dos

1 1-ounce package taco seasoning mix
1 8-ounce container sour cream.

Mix ingredients. Serve with tortilla or corn chips. Makes 1 cup.

The Incredible Pesto-Brie Spread

1 unit of Brie cheese, wedge or round
1 4-ounce container of pesto

Place brie on an oven-safe serving platter or dish. Cut rind off top of brie, but don't remove sides or bottom (rind will keep brie from sticking to platter). Spread ¼ to ½ cup pesto over brie. Bake at 350 degrees for 10 minutes for a wedge of brie, 15 minutes for a round. Watch *CAREFULLY*. Remove from oven with oven mitts. Serve with crackers, sour dough baguette slices, or French bread.

Creamy Fruit Dip

> **1 3.4-ounce package Jell-O French Vanilla pudding mix**
>
> **2 cups heavy cream**

Combine pudding mix and heavy cream. Mixture will thicken in 5 minutes. Dip pieces of fresh fruit (strawberries, cantaloupe, mango, etc.) into mixture. Especially terrific with bananas. Equally wonderful on plain crackers, vegetables or clean fingers. Makes 2½ cups. Recipe can be halved.

Hot Bean Dip

> **1 16-ounce can refried beans**
>
> **½ cup Pace Picante Sauce, or your favorite salsa**

Combine ingredients in a medium saucepan until heated, stirring occasionally. Or place in microwave-safe bowl and heat on medium-high for 1 minute. Serve with tortilla chips.

Mild Bean Dip

> **1 8-ounce jar spicy bean dip**
>
> **1 8-ounce container sour cream**

Combine bean dip and sour cream until smooth. Serve with tortilla or corn chips.

Creamy Salsa Dip

> **1 8-ounce container whipped cream cheese, room temperature**
>
> **½ cup salsa**

Combine ingredients. Makes 1½ cups. Serve with tortilla chips or cut-up vegetables.

South of the Border Dip

 1 15-ounce can chili without beans

 1 8-ounce package cream cheese, cut into 1-inch pieces

Microwave method: Place cream cheese in microwave-safe dish and top with chili; cover. Heat on high for 1 minute. Stir mixture and heat on high for 1 minute; stir again.

Stovetop method: Place both ingredients into a medium saucepan and warm over medium heat, stirring occasionally, until cream cheese melts. Pour into small serving dish and serve with tortilla chips. Makes 2 cups.

Cheesy Salsa Dip

 1 pound Velveeta cheese spread (found in the dairy case or with snack items)

 1 8-ounce jar Pace Picante Sauce, or your favorite salsa

Combine salsa and chunks of Velveeta in a medium saucepan. Stir over low heat until cheese has melted. Serve with tortilla chips or vegetable spears (carrot, celery, zucchini, and/or bell peppers) for dipping. Mixture can also be microwaved in microwave-safe bowl on high for 5 minutes. Makes 3 cups.

Variation: Substitute regular Velveeta for Mexican-Style Velveeta.

Cream Cheese and Friends Dip

 1 8-ounce package regular or low-fat cream cheese, room temperature

 ½ cup of one of the following: pepper jelly, Pace Picante Sauce, or chutney

Place unwrapped cream cheese on a serving dish. Pour either pepper jelly, sauce or chutney over the cream cheese. Serve with crackers.

Great Guacamole

> **3 avocados**
>
> **1/3 cup Pace Picante Sauce**
>
> **1 squeeze of lemon juice to prevent avocado from turning brown, optional**

Split avocados lengthwise. Peel and remove pits. Mash avocado in a medium bowl. Add 1/3 cup Pace Picante Sauce; combine. Serve with taco chips. Makes 1½ cups.

Milder version: Add 1 or 2 tablespoons sour cream to the mixture.

Tip to soften under-ripe avocado: Pierce avocado once or twice, place on an upside-down saucer and microwave, uncovered, on high 30 to 60 seconds, turning over and rotating ½ turn at half time, until warm. Cool and peel.

Easy Generic Dip

> **1 10-ounce can cheddar cheese soup**
>
> **½ cup canned beef broth**

Empty cheese soup into medium saucepan. Stir in beef broth. Heat and stir, or whisk over medium heat until warm. Serve with pre-made meatballs (found in the freezer case) or chunks of French bread. Makes 1½ cups.

Mystery Dip for Meatballs

> **8 ounces currant jelly**
>
> **5 tablespoons Dijon mustard**

In a small bowl, combine jelly and mustard, beating with a wire whisk. Specks of jelly will dissolve in 5 minutes for a smooth dip. Serve with: pre-made meatballs (found in the freezer case). Also good on sandwiches. Makes 1 cup.

Three-Ingredient Hot Artichoke Dip

1 14-ounce can artichokes

1 cup grated Parmesan cheese

1 cup mayonnaise

Drain artichokes and chop coarsely. Add Parmesan cheese and mayonnaise. Place in a 1-quart baking dish and bake at 350 degrees until bubbly, about 20 minutes. Serve with corn ships, crackers or raw vegetables. Serves 6 to 8.

Variation: Add 1 4-ounce can chopped chiles.

Jamaican Surprise

1 3-ounce package cream cheese, room temperature

¼ cup Pickapeppa sauce (found at the grocer near steak sauce)

Let cream cheese soften about ½ hour (or soften in microwave oven for 1 minute on medium low). Place cream cheese on serving platter and cover with Pickapeppa sauce. Serve with crackers to spread.

California Crab Dip

1 6-ounce can crabmeat, drained, or 1 cup fresh, cooked crabmeat

2-3 tablespoons barbecue sauce

Drain crabmeat and combine with barbecue sauce. Add a squeeze of fresh lemon, if desired. Serve with crackers.

Cold Crustacean Appetizer Dip

> **1 cup seafood salad, purchased at a delicatessen**
>
> **1 teaspoon curry powder**

Mince salad with a knife. Add curry and mix well. Pour into a serving container and refrigerate until ready to serve with crackers.

Variation: Serve spread on round slices of peeled cucumbers.

Shrimpy Dip

> **3 4-ounce seafood (shrimp or crab) cocktails, chilled**
>
> **1 8-ounce package cream cheese, softened to room temperature**

Combine ingredients in a blender. Serve with crackers or corn chips.

Variation: Simply pour 2 seafood cocktails over the brick of cream cheese.

Items to Dip

- **bagel chips**
- **bell peppers**
- **broccoli florets**
- **carrot sticks**
- **cauliflowerets**
- **celery sticks**
- **cucumber strips**
- **crusty French or Italian bread chunks**
- **endive scoops**
- **miniature yellow and green pattypan squash**
- **mushrooms**
- **prepared frozen meatballs (thawed and heated)**

- radishes
- string beans
- sugar peas
- tomatoes
- turnip sticks
- zucchini strips

Bonus points: Crisp raw vegetables in ice water, dry and sprinkle with seasoned salt. Arrange vegetables in a small wicker basket à la Martha Stewart. Serve dips in hollowed out mini-pumpkins, heads of cabbage, or bell peppers.

ॐ Small-Bites/Appetizers ॐ

Chived Cheese

¼ pound feta cheese

1 bunch chives, finely chopped

Cut feta cheese into cubes. Chop fresh chives. Roll cheese in chives. Spear with toothpicks, if desired, or serve herbed cheese atop a lettuce leaf. Serves 4.

Variation: Substitute chopped parsley or green onion tops for chives.

'Some Like it Hot' Jerk Chicken

1 package chicken wings or drumettes

½ teaspoon jerk seasoning (Jamaican dry mix seasoning)

Rinse chicken parts and put in a bowl. Add jerk spice. Mix well to coat chicken. Place chicken on broiler pan. Bake for 20-30 minutes at 350 degrees.

Tip: Eating dairy products with plenty of fat, such as sour cream, milk, or yogurt, will dampen the spice fire.

Chicken Little Lite Bites (the calories are falling...)

> **1 skinless chicken breast cutlet (about 4 ounces)**
>
> **2 tablespoons cornmeal**
>
> **1 tablespoon low- or non-fat milk, optional**

Preheat oven to 350 degrees. Spray a baking pan with non-stick vegetable spray. Rinse and dry chicken. Slice chicken into strips. Dip in water, or milk, if using, and coat with cornmeal. Bake for approximately 20 minutes. Serve with salsa dipping sauce, if desired.

Dipping Sauces for Chicken

- **Combine ¼ cup honey and ¼ cup spicy brown mustard.**
- **Combine ¼ cup marmalade with ¼ cup hot prepared mustard.**
- **Combine 1/3 cup sour cream and 1/3 cup Dijon mustard.**
- **Combine 1/3 cup mayonnaise and 1 teaspoon curry powder.**
- **Combine 1/3 cup mayonnaise and 1-2 finely chopped garlic cloves.**
- **Combine 1/3 cup barbecue sauce and 1 tablespoon catsup.**

Note: These will really grow on you. You've been warned.

Al's Dogs

> **1 12-ounce package of smokie links**
>
> **1 8-ounce container of refrigerator crescent rolls**

Remove rolls from package. Wrap 1 crescent roll around each smokie link. Place on an oven-safe platter or ungreased cookie sheet. Bake at 375 degrees for 11-15 minutes. Makes 8. Serve with assorted mustards. And beer. At a poker game.

Diablo Eggs

6 hard-boiled eggs

1/3 cup Pace Picante Sauce, or your favorite salsa

To cook eggs: Place eggs in saucepan and cover with water; bring to a boil over medium heat. Reduce heat to low and let simmer for 20 minutes. Remove eggs and rinse with cold water, or just pour cold water into the pan.

Peel cooled eggs; cut in half. Remove and mash yolks. Blend in picante sauce. Refill whites. Chill. Makes 12 appetizers.

Pickled Eggs

6 hard-boiled eggs

1 32-ounce bottle white vinegar

To cook eggs: Place eggs in saucepan and cover with water; bring to a boil over medium heat. Reduce heat to low and let simmer for 20 minutes. Remove eggs and rinse with cold water, or just pour cold water into the pan.

Peel cooled eggs. Pour half of the vinegar into a large jar with a non-corrosive lid. (Plastic containers with lids are ideal.) Drop the eggs into the container and cover with the remaining vinegar. Put the lid on the jar and store in the refrigerator.

Variation: Add ½ cup halved or quartered small white onions.

Quesadillas

4 flour tortillas

6 ounces Sharp Cheddar Cheese or Monterey Jack Cheese, grated

1 tablespoon olive oil

Sprinkle cheese in center of 2 tortillas. Spread cheese almost to edges. Top each with remaining tortillas. Heat 1 tablespoon oil in a large skillet. Place 1 quesadilla sandwich in skillet and fry until crisp, turn and fry the other side. Drain well on paper towel and place in a warm oven while frying the other quesadilla. Cut into quarters. Serve with salsa and sour cream, if desired. Makes 8 wedges.

Insanely-Delicious Couldn't-Be-Easier Hors d'oeuvres

8 ounces hot pepper Jack cheese

1 package won ton wrappers (available in the refrigerated produce section, near the Asian vegetables, at the grocer's)

Cut pepper cheese into small squares the size of a sugar cube. Using an ungreased miniature muffin tin, fit 1 won ton wrapper into each opening. Drop a cube of hot pepper cheese into each indentation. Bake approximately 6 to 8 minutes in a 350-degree oven until the cheese melts and the wrappers crisp and turn golden. Makes 24-36.

Filling Variations

- 1 teaspoon sautéed mushrooms topped with 1 tablespoon Brie cheese

- 2 tablespoons Gruyere cheese and 1 teaspoon chopped chives

- frozen peas and chopped prosciutto

- 4 ounces deviled ham combined with 2 ounces light cream cheese

- Velveeta or Cheese Whiz and chopped olives
- pesto and Parmesan cheese
- herb & garlic spreadable cheese
- frozen pre-cooked meatballs (thawed) and bottled pizza sauce

Prosciutto-Wrapped Asparagus

12-24 asparagus spears

6-12 thin slices prosciutto (available from delicatessens)

Cut off the large ends from the asparagus to leave 6-inch tips. In a large pan, bring 1 inch of water to boil over high heat. Add the asparagus and cook until just tender, 3 to 4 minutes. Remove from water and rinse under cold water. Drain well, allow to cool and pat dry. If prosciutto slices are wide, cut each slice in half horizontally and roll around an asparagus spear. Arrange on a serving platter. Makes 12-24.

Variations

- *Vegetable Wraps:* wrap prosciutto around raw zucchini spears, canned baby corn on the cob, cucumber spears, or blanched tiny red potatoes
- *Fruit Wraps:* wrap prosciutto around rip fig halves, cantaloupe, or papaya wedges
- *Bread Wraps:* wrap prosciutto around breadsticks
- *Meat Wraps:* wrap prosciutto around browned chicken

Sauce suggestion: Mix 2/3 cup mayonnaise and 2 tablespoons orange juice.

Broiled BBQ Shrimp

24 frozen cooked shrimp

¾ cup bottled BBQ sauce

Place shrimp in a foil-lined pan; brush shrimp with sauce. Broil 3 minutes. Turn and brush shrimp with more sauce. Broil 2 additional minutes. Serve with toothpicks.

Shrimp on a Stick

1 pound cleaned, peeled and cooked shrimp

½ cup vinaigrette dressing

Place shrimp into a medium size bowl. Pour dressing over shrimp and stir. Cover and marinate in refrigerator for 2-4 hours, turning occasionally. Skewer with toothpicks and serve.

Variations: Wrap each shrimp with prosciutto and skewer. Substitute pesto for vinaigrette.

Cold Vegetables and Friends

- **Raw mushroom caps filled with herbed spreadable cheese, deviled ham or pâté**
- **Anchovy fillets wrapped around red radishes**
- **Canned artichoke bottoms filled with liver pâté or cheese spread**

Buttered Pecans

1 cup pecan halves, shelled

¼ cup butter, melted

Preheat oven to 400 degrees. Spread the pecans in a baking dish. Drizzle with melted butter. Stir pecans or shake dish to cover pecans with butter. Bake for 10 minutes for a delicious toasted flavor.

Salami Stuffing

1 whole dried salami

2 8-ounce packages low-fat cream cheese

Hollow out a French bread roll, leaving some bread inside the crust. Grind up salami and mix with cream cheese until smooth. Stuff the mixture into the hollowed-out loaf. Wrap the loaf with foil and freeze. Remove roll from freezer the night before serving and leave in the refrigerator overnight. Slice roll while bread is still cold and hard. Makes 24 rounds.

Sausage and Mushroom Caps

1 10-ounce tube seasoned sausage

2 dozen mushrooms

Spray a baking pan with non-stick vegetable spray. Rinse and dry mushrooms; remove stems by pulling them out to create a cavity for the sausage. Place a spoonful of sausage on each mushroom cap. Place in oven and bake for 30-40 minutes at 350 degrees; or broil for 5-6 minutes. Makes 2 dozen.

3

Snacks

Instant Apple Pie

1 flour tortilla

¼ cup canned apple pie filling

Place filling down the center of the tortilla; roll up jelly-roll fashion. Heat on high 1 minute in a microwave oven, or bake in an oven for 5 minutes at 350 degrees.

Cheese Pockets

1 8-ounce can refrigerated crescent rolls

1 cup shredded sharp cheddar cheese

Preheat oven to 375 degrees. Unroll dough and separate into 4 rectangles; don't separate at the triangle perforations. Pinch the triangle perforations to seal. Press each rectangle to enlarge to 7x5 inches. Place ¼ cup shredded cheese on half of each rectangle. Fold dough in half over filling and pinch edges to seal. Place on an ungreased cookie sheet and bake for 10 to 15 minutes. Makes 4 sandwich pockets.

Jam Pockets

1 8-ounce package refrigerated biscuits

½ cup jam, your favorite flavor

Separate biscuits and flatten with a fork until you've doubled their size. Place a tablespoon of jam in the middle of each roll; fold over and seal with a fork around the edges. Sprinkle tops with sugar, if desired. Bake on an ungreased cookie sheet in a 375-degree oven for 12-16 minutes or until browned. Makes 3-4 servings.

Chocolate Cream Snack Spread

¼ cup soft cream cheese

1 2-ounce milk chocolate bar (broken into pieces) or ¼ cup chocolate chips

Toast 2 slices of bread or a split bagel. Place ½ of the chocolate on the still-hot toasted surfaces. Spread cream cheese on top of chocolate, top with remaining chocolate. Ooooh, baby!

PBR Spread

½ cup chunky peanut butter

¼ cup raisins, finely chopped

Mix ingredients well. Spread on toast, toasted bagels or muffin halves. Makes ¾ cup.

Quick Mexican Pizza

1 corn tortilla

¼ cup shredded Monterey Jack cheese

Microwave tortilla on a paper towel on high for 3 minutes, or until crisp. Place tortilla on a microwave-safe plate and top with cheese. Microwave on high for 1 minute, or until cheese melts. Serves 1.

Variations: Top cheese with 2 tablespoons taco sauce and/or 1 tablespoon canned chopped chiles.

Creamy Tortilla Filling

1 tablespoon jalapeño or salsa Cheez Whiz

1 tablespoon low-fat cream cheese

Spread 1 flour tortilla with Cheez Whiz, then spread with cream cheese. Roll up and cut into 6 snack-size rolls. Serves 1.

Low-Fat Tortilla Chips

1 package uncooked corn or flour tortillas

¼ teaspoon salt or Mexican seasoning, optional

Cut tortillas into quarters. Dip pieces in water; place them in a single layer on a cookie sheet. Bake in a 375-degree oven until crisp, about 10 minutes. Turn them over a couple of times during cooking, sprinkle with salt or Mexican seasoning, if using. Serve with salsa, if desired.

Chocolate Roll-Ups

1 8-ounce container refrigerated crescent dinner rolls

1 cup milk chocolate chips

Preheat oven to 400 degrees. Unroll dough and separate into 4 rectangles (don't separate dough at the triangle perforations). Place ¼ of the chocolate chips on 1 narrow end of each rectangle, then roll up jelly-roll fashion. Pinch ends closed to make sure chocolate doesn't ooze out. Arrange the 4 rolls with seam side down on an ungreased cookie sheet. Bake for 18 to 20 minutes until golden. Serve at room temperature. Makes 4 rolls.

Variation: Sift powdered sugar over rolls.

Sweet Coating for Tortillas

¼ teaspoon sugar

¼ teaspoon cinnamon

Sprinkle 1 side of 4 flour tortillas with sugar, then cinnamon. Place on a cookie sheet. Bake in oven for 1 hour at 200 degrees. Break into pieces to eat. Serves 2.

Packable Tortilla Roll-ups (Roll your own before you hike or camp)

Fillings

- jelly
- peanut butter
- deviled ham
- cheese
- tuna salad

Spread fillings on tortillas and roll up, or take ingredients with you and make the roll-ups on-site when camping or hiking.

4

Soups

Lighting Fast Borscht

1 8-ounce can beets, drained

1 8-ounce can tomatoes

Purée drained beets and undrained tomatoes in a blender. Ladle into a bowl. Enjoy this soup cold on a hot day, or try the heated variation below. Serves 4.

Variation: Add 1 10-ounce can chicken broth to the mixture and heat. Garnish with 1 tablespoon yogurt or sour cream.

Creamy Borscht

1 16-ounce can beets, reserve ½ the juice

1 8-ounce container light sour cream

Place beets, half the beet juice, and sour cream in a blender and purée until smooth, about 2 minutes. Chill for at least 2 hours before serving. Serves 4.

Velvety Cheddar Soup

1 10-ounce can cheddar cheese soup

1 10-ounce can beef broth

Combine ingredients in a medium saucepan and heat. Do not add water. Do not boil. Serves 2-3.

Soup in Edible Bread Bowls

> **2 round Italian breads, 7-inch diameter**
>
> **1 19-ounce can clam chowder, or cream of spinach soup**

Cut tops off round bread loaves. To create a hollowed-out bowl, cut circle near perimeter of bread, careful not to cut through to bottom. Scoop out interior bread. Fill bread bowls with heated soup, prepared according to directions on can. When you've finished eating the soup, tear your bread bowl into chunks and enjoy it with a salad, if desired. Serves 2.

Optional: Place hollowed-out loaves and bread 'lids' on a cookie sheet or rack; bake in a 425-degree oven for 8 minutes or until slightly toasted. *CAUTION:* Soup will be *very hot* if eaten from pre-heated bread bowls.

Variation: Fill with bread bowls with chili and top with cheddar cheese.

Curry Carrot Soup

> **1 16-ounce bag frozen cut carrots, or 3-4 carrots, cut into 1-inch chunks**
>
> **2 10-ounce cans chicken broth (1 of which is a low-sodium/low-fat version)**
>
> **¼ to ½ teaspoon curry powder, depending upon how much you like curry**

In a medium saucepan, combine ingredients and bring to a boil over medium-high heat. Cover, reduce heat to low and simmer 15-20 minutes. Let cool 10 minutes. Purée in a blender. Serves 2-3.

Variation: After the ingredients have been puréed, stir in ¾ cup low-fat plain yogurt.

Hearty Chili Soup

1 15-ounce can turkey chili with beans

1 10-ounce can beef broth

¼ teaspoon ground cumin, optional

Combine chili, broth, and cumin, if using, in a medium saucepan and heat. Serves 2-3.

Variations: Add 1 4-ounce can Mexican-style corn, drained. Top with salsa, crushed corn chips, plain yogurt or sour cream, if desired.

Indian Curry Soup

1 10-ounce can chicken broth

½ teaspoon curry power

purchased croutons, optional

Bring broth to a boil and add curry powder. Top with croutons, if using. Serves 2.

Variation: Whisk in 1 tablespoon grated Parmesan cheese.

Pasta Soup

1 49-ounce can chicken broth

1 12-ounce package fresh or frozen tortellini (filled with cheese, chicken or meat)

Pour the broth into a medium saucepan. Over high heat, bring the broth to a boil. Add the tortellini and follow the package directions, until the pasta is tender, 6-7 minutes. Serves 4.

Variations: Add ½ cup fresh chopped spinach leaves during the last minutes of cooking. Top soup with Parmesan cheese.

Note: If you leave the can of broth in the refrigerator for a few hours, the fat will be solidified and is easily removed.

Rush Hour Green Chili Soup

> 1 19-ounce can chunky chicken corn chowder soup,
> undiluted, or chunky cream of chicken soup, undiluted
>
> 1 4-ounce can diced green chiles, drained

Drain chiles. Combine contents of both cans in a medium saucepan and heat. Do not add water or other liquid. Very spicy! Serves 3.

Amazingly Good Watercress Soup

> 2 10-ounce cans chicken broth (1 of which is a low-sodium version)
>
> 2 cups watercress sprigs (1 large bunch), rinsed and drained well

In a medium saucepan, bring broth to a boil over high heat. Add rinsed and drained watercress; cover and simmer until watercress is tender to the bite, 2 to 3 minutes. *IMPORTANT:* Remove soup from heat for 10 minutes and let cool before pouring into blender. Otherwise, placing molten soup into a blender and immediately starting it up will give you the feeling of standing at the rim of a volcano. Purée the mixture in a blender, a portion at a time. Season to taste with pepper, if desired. Serve warm. (This is a great soup for a thermos.) Or cover and chill up to 1 day and serve cold. Serves 2.

Variation: For a delightfully tart flavor, add ¼ cup low-fat yogurt or sour cream during the blender process.

Sneaky Veggie Soup (An easy way to sneak vegetables into veggiphobics)

1 10-ounce can chicken broth

½ to 1 cup of any combination roasted, steamed or microwaved vegetables, puréed

Purée cooked vegetables with ½ cup water. Add purée to simmering broth for a creamy soup. Serves 2.

Note: Amazingly delicious when roasted vegetables are used. See Roasted Vegetable recipe.

5

Salads

Green Salad Supplements

To a basic salad of greens add another ingredient, such as:

- **avocado slices**
- **artichoke hearts, marinated**
- **baby corn**
- **bean sprouts**
- **beet slices**
- **carrot shavings**
- **celery (cut at a 45-degree angle to avoid stringiness)**
- **cheese strips or shreds**
- **corn kernels**
- **croutons**
- **cooked egg slices**
- **edible flowers**
- **kidney beans**
- **hominy**
- **mushrooms**
- **orange slices**
- **radish slices**
- **raisins**
- **sunflower seeds**
- **tomato wedges**

Avocado Dressing

1 avocado, divided use

½ cup of your favorite vinaigrette dressing

Cut avocado lengthwise and remove pit. Combine ½ avocado with the dressing in a blender until smooth. Slice remaining avocado for use in the salad.

Tip: To keep avocados from turning brown, add a little squeeze of lemon.

Avocado and Mango Salad

1 avocado

1 mango

1 splash of fresh lime juice, optional

Slice fruit in half lengthwise. Remove skins. Place alternating slices of avocado and mango on 2 salad plates. Splash with lime juice, if desired. Serves 2.

Fruit Salad Dressing

½ cup low-fat sour cream

¼ cup preserves (strawberry, blackberry, etc.)

Combine ingredients and pour over melon, berries, peaches or other fruit.

Wild Carrot Salad

2-3 carrots, shredded (or purchased pre-shredded carrots)

2 tablespoons Italian or vinaigrette dressing

Rinse and shred carrots. Toss with dressing. Serves 2.

Variation: Fat-free Italian Parmesan or Ranch dressing.

Melon Mix

1 cantaloupe

2 tablespoons Midori melon liquor

Remove rind and cut melon into pieces, place in serving dishes. Splash on the Midori! Serves 2.

Variation: Add additional fruit, such as raspberries, blackberries, honeydew melon, mango, mandarin oranges, papaya, banana, and/or kiwi.

Parsley Salad

2 cups salad greens

¼ cup chopped parsley

Mix and top with your favorite salad dressing. Serves 2.

3-Bean Boats

1 15-ounce jar or can marinated 3-bean salad

4 tomatoes

Rinse and dry tomatoes. With a sharp knife, cut off the stem end of the tomatoes ½ inch from the top; remove the cores. Place the tomatoes on a paper towel, cut end down. Cutting to within ½ inch of the bottom, make 4 cuts into each tomato to create a circle with 8 wedges. Carefully spread the wedges to open; top each tomato with ½ cup drained 3-bean salad. Serves 4.

Variation: Serve marinated beans in a halved and pitted avocado.

6

Irresistible Breads and Spreads

Crunchy Parmesan Bread

8 slices French or sourdough bread

¼ cup grated Parmesan cheese

Lightly toast bread slices in a 350-degree oven or oven toaster until bread starts to turn a light brown. Remove bread from heat and sprinkle with grated Parmesan cheese. Return to heat. Remove bread when it starts to turn golden, about 1 minute. Serves 4.

Cheesy Guest Bread Spread

½ cup mayonnaise

½ cup grated Parmesan cheese

Combine mayonnaise and Parmesan cheese. Spread over horizontally-sliced French loaf. Bake at 350 degrees for 10 minutes.

Variation: Spread mixture on small cocktail breads, bake for 5 minutes and serve as hors d'oeuvres. Serves 6.

Drunk Bread

1 12-ounce can beer

3 cups self-rising flour (Gold Medal makes this, as well as other companies)

2 tablespoons sugar

Mix ingredients together until blended. Pour into a greased 9x5x3-inch loaf pan. Bake at 350 degrees for 1 hour.

Dream Biscuits

> 1 cup self-rising flour (Gold Medal makes this, as well as
>   other companies)
>
> 1 cup heavy/whipping cream
>
> 2 tablespoons sugar

Preheat oven to 400 degrees. Grease or spray mini- or regular muffin
tins with a non-stick coating. Mix ingredients in a large bowl and
pour into muffin cups. Bake mini-muffins for 15 minutes; bake
regular-size muffins for 25 minutes or until tops are lightly browned.
Makes 24 mini- or 12 regular muffins.

Garlic Bread Spread

> 1 4-ounce container Alouette Light garlic and herb
>   spreadable cheese
>
> ¼ cup Parmesan cheese

Spread cheese over sliced French bread. Sprinkle with Parmesan
cheese. Bake at 425 degrees for 4-5 minutes, or broil until cheese
melts. Serves 6.

Garlic Toast Spread

> 1 large garlic clove, minced
>
> ¼ cup olive oil

In a small skillet, cook garlic in oil over medium-low heat, stirring,
until garlic begins to turn golden, about 1 minute. Cut a baguette or
French loaf lengthwise, then into large serving pieces; brush with oil
from skillet. Place bread in 375-degree oven for 10 minutes, or until
golden. Serves 6.

Garlic Butter Spread

2 cloves garlic, crushed

4 tablespoons softened butter

Combine 4 tablespoons softened butter and 2 cloves of garlic, crushed. Spread the mixture on each side of a loaf of French bread, sliced lengthwise. Arrange bread on a cookie sheet and toast under broiler for 2-3 minutes, watching carefully, or heat in a 375-degree oven for 10-12 minutes.

Variation: Add a topping of 4 tablespoons grated Parmesan cheese.

4-Star Onion Bread Spread

½ stick (¼ cup) butter

¼ package dry onion soup mix

Soften butter and mix with onion soup mix. Split a French bread loaf in half lengthwise. Spread the butter mixture over each cut side. Bake bread halves for 20 minutes at 350 degrees. Serves 6. Get ready for the applause.

Pesto Bread

1 7-ounce container pesto (a thick, green basil sauce used for pasta; find it shelved with refrigerated pasta sauces or in the freezer)

1 package pre-sliced sour dough bread, or 1 loaf of French bread, sliced

Lightly toast bread slices in a toaster oven or 350-degree oven for 10 minutes, or until bread has just started to turn a light brown. Remove bread from heat and spread with pesto. Serves many!

7

Main Courses

Spicy Burrito Filling

> **1 pound stew meat, cut into 2-inch squares**
>
> **1 16-ounce jar Pace Picante Sauce, or your favorite salsa**

In a medium skillet, cook meat over medium heat for 10-14 minutes until brown. Place browned meat in a crockpot and pour Picante Sauce over the meat. Cover and cook on low 6 to 8 hours, or on high for 4 hours. Remove meat from sauce, shred, and return shredded meat to sauce to simmer for 10 minutes. Ladle ¼ cup filling in the center of each warmed flour tortilla. Serves 4.

Note: Warm tortillas in microwave oven for 30 seconds each, or in 350-degree oven for 4-7 minutes.

Two-Minute Burrito Filling

> **1 15-ounce can chili without beans**
>
> **1 8-ounce package cream cheese, cut into 1-inch pieces**

Microwave method: Place cream cheese in a microwave-safe dish and top with chili; cover. Heat on high for 1 minute. Stir mixture; heat on high for 1 additional minute. Stir again and place filling in warmed flour burritos.

Stovetop method: Pour chili into medium saucepan, top with cream cheese. Heat on medium until cheese is melted, stirring often.

Variation: Add ½ cup cheddar cheese during the heating process.

Note: Warm burritos in a microwave oven by placing them between 2 lightly dampened paper towels. Heat on high for 30 seconds each.

Like-You-Cooked-It-for-Hours Chili

1 15-ounce can chili with beans

1 15-ounce can pinto beans, drained

Combine ingredients in a medium saucepan. Heat over medium flame until warm. Serves 3.

Variations: Top chili with grated cheddar cheese, diced onions, or crushed corn chips.

ABC Stew

½ pound ground hamburger

1 10-ounce can alphabet soup

In a medium saucepan, brown hamburger, then drain oil. Add alphabet soup; don't add water. Heat until soup is warm. Serves 2.

EZ Pizza

1 10-ounce container refrigerated Pillsbury All Ready Pizza Crust (found in the grocer's refrigerated roll section)

1 14-ounce jar or can pizza sauce

Follow directions for preparing pizza dough on container. Follow tips such as pre-baking crust for crispness, and greasing pizza pan or 13 x 9-inch pan with 1 tablespoon vegetable oil and 1 tablespoon cornmeal. Top pre-baked dough with 1 cup pizza sauce. Total baking time: 15-25 minutes. And fresher than a 'pizza place' version. Serve with a green salad. Serves 2.

Variations: Top with Parmesan cheese, sliced olives, leftover roasted vegetables or meat.

Skillet Chops and Wild Rice

4 loin pork chops

1 6-ounce package long grain and wild rice mix

Spray a large skillet with non-stick vegetable spray. Brown pork chops on both sides in large skillet over medium high heat, moving meat around in the skillet occasionally so that it doesn't weld to the pan. Remove chops and set aside. In the same skillet, combine rice, seasoning pack ingredients, and water according to package directions; bring to a boil. Arrange chops on rice mixture. Reduce heat; cover and simmer 20 to 25 minutes, or until pork chops are no longer pink. Makes 4 servings.

Pork Chops and Creamy Rice

4 or 5 boneless loin pork chops

1 10-ounce can chicken-rice soup

Spray medium skillet with a non-stick vegetable spray. If desired, season pork chops with salt and pepper. Brown pork chops on both sides over medium high heat; remove chops and place in a crock pot. Pour chicken-rice soup over the pork chops and cook on low 6 to 8 hours. Makes 4-5 servings.

Oven Pork Chops and Corn

4 pork chops, with or without bones

2 15-ounce cans corn (1 regular style corn, drained; and 1 cream-style)

Preheat oven to 350 degrees. Butter or spray a 2-quart baking dish with non-stick vegetable spray. Pour corn into dish and combine, then top with pork chops. Salt and pepper to taste. Bake for 25-30 minutes. Serves 4-5.

Golden Pork Chops

>   **4 boneless loin pork chops**
>
>   **1 10-ounce can golden mushroom soup (cream of
>   mushroom soup may be substituted)**
>
>   **1 tablespoon flour, optional**

Spray medium skillet with non-stick vegetable spray. If using, dust chops with flour, and season with salt and pepper. Brown pork chops on both sides over medium high heat; remove chops and set aside. Remove oil, if any. In same skillet, combine soup and ½ cup water. Return chops to skillet. Reduce heat; cover and simmer 45 minutes, stirring occasionally. Makes 4 servings.

Variation: Chops can be browned then transferred with soup mixture to oven. Bake at 350 degrees for 1 hour.

Easiest Pork Roast

>   **1 3 to 4 pound pork roast**
>   **2 27-ounce can sauerkraut**

Pour 1 can of sauerkraut into a 9x13-inch roasting pan. Place roast on top. Pour another can of sauerkraut over roast. Rinse cans with a splash of water; pour water over the roast. Cover and cook at 325 to 350 degrees for about 3 hours, or until the roast is tender. Serve with mashed potatoes and rye bread. Serves 6.

Countrystyle Crockpot Porkribs

>   **2 pounds countrystyle porkribs**
>   **1 27-ounce can sauerkraut**

Place porkribs in crockpot. Pour sauerkraut over porkribs. Rinse can with ¼ cup water and add to crockpot. Cover and cook on low 6 to 8 hours. A great way to have dinner ready the moment you get home. Serves 4.

Brisket Thompson

> **3 to 4 pound brisket**
>
> **1 2-ounce envelope onion soup mix**
>
> **½ cup wine, optional**

Place brisket in a covered roasting pan. Combine soup mix with 1½ cups water, plus ½ cup wine, if using. Pour over brisket. Cover and roast at 325 to 350 degrees for 3½ hours. Check every hour, add water if liquid has evaporated. Serves 4.

Variation: Add 1 sliced onion to the bottom of the pan, under the brisket. Add 1 pound scrubbed baby potatoes and/or carrots to pan during last 1½ hours.

Crockpot Brisket

> **3 pound brisket**
>
> **1 2-ounce envelope onion soup mix**

Place brisket in the crockpot and top with onion soup mix. Do not add any liquid. Cook on low for 6-8 hours. Serves 4.

Dijon Beef

> **1½ pound beef tenderloin roast**
>
> **3 tablespoons Dijon mustard**

Preheat oven to 425 degrees. Spread mustard over top of roast; sprinkle with black pepper, if desired. Place beef in a roasting pan. Bake for 60 minutes or until meat thermometer registers 140 degrees for rare, 160 degrees for medium. Remove roast from oven and let rest for 10 minutes before slicing. Serves 4-5.

Overnight-Sensation Marinade for Flank Steak

¼ cup red wine

¼ cup soy sauce

Combine wine and soy sauce in a shallow dish. Marinate 1½ pounds flank steak for at least 1 hour, turning occasionally, or marinate overnight. Grill flank steak (5 minutes for medium rare), basting with marinade, until done. Do not baste during last few minutes of cooking. Slice in thin slices across the grain. Serves 2.

Variation: Substitute ½ cup Italian dressing for wine and soy sauce mixture.

Easy Gravy for Pot Roast

1 2-ounce package dry onion soup mix

1 10-ounce can golden mushroom soup

Place a 3 pound roast on a large piece of foil. Sprinkle dry onion soup mix over roast; cover with mushroom soup. Completely seal roast with foil. Bake at 350 degrees for 3 hours. Serves 4-6.

Barbecue Beef Sandwich Filling

1½ pound roast or brisket

½ bottle barbecue sauce

Rinse beef, pat dry and place in bottom of crockpot. Pour barbecue sauce over beef. Cover and cook on low for 8-10 hours. Serve over toasted hamburger buns or steak rolls. Serves 6. Serve with a green salad and a big beverage, and no one will go hungry!

Meatloaf Madness

1½ pounds hamburger, or ground turkey

1 7-ounce box of your favorite stuffing mix, plus seasoning packet

Preheat oven to 375 degrees. Combine stuffing mix with seasoning in a large bowl, add ¾ cup water, and stir. Add ground meat and mix well. Pour into an ungreased 9x5x3-inch loaf pan. Bake for 1 hour. Serves 6-8.

Meatball Sauce

1 bag frozen meatballs

1 15-ounce can or jar spaghetti sauce

Place 6 frozen meatballs *per person* into a crockpot. Pour the entire container of spaghetti sauce over the meatballs. Cook on low 6 to 8 hours. Serve over cooked pasta or toasted French rolls for sandwiches. Serves a small crowd.

❧ Chicken and Turkey ❧

Almost-Instant Barbecue Chicken

2 chicken breasts

½ cup bottled barbecue sauce

Wash and pat dry chicken. Cut chicken into 4-6 strips. Spray a medium skillet with non-stick vegetable spray, or add 1 teaspoon butter, if desired. Sauté chicken breasts over medium heat. After chicken is lightly browned, pour the barbecue sauce over it and sauté for 2-3 minutes. Serves 2.

Baked Barbecue Chicken

>   **8 skinless chicken pieces**
>   **1 cup bottled barbecue sauce**
>   **2 tablespoons flour**

Note: You'll need 1 baking bag (found in the plastic wrap section of the grocery store)

Preheat oven to 400 degrees. Rinse chicken and pat dry. Throw flour into baking bag and shake. Add barbecue sauce to bag. Squeeze bag to blend ingredients. Sprinkle chicken with salt and pepper, if desired; place chicken in bag. Turn bag to coat chicken with sauce. Arrange chicken in an even layer. Put tie wrap around open end of bag; place bag into 13x9x2-inch baking pan. Cut a small hole in middle of bag. Place pan in oven and bake for 45-50 minutes. *Remember to cut a hole in the bag.* Serves 4.

Crunchy Baked Coating for Chicken

>   **1 10-ounce jar chicken gravy, ½ cup used for coating chicken**
>   **1 10-ounce package seasoned croutons, crushed**
>   **2-3 tablespoons butter, melted**

Preheat oven to 375 degrees. Rinse and dry 2 pounds of chicken legs, breasts, or thighs with paper towels. Crush croutons by opening the package and running a heavy object over the bag. Dip chicken in ½ cup gravy, then in croutons to coat. Place chicken in a baking dish or pan that has been sprayed with vegetable coating, if desired. Drizzle chicken with 2 tablespoons butter. Bake for 1 hour. Remove chicken from pan and keep warm. Pour remaining gravy in pan, stir up brown bits, and return to oven for 2-3 minutes. Serve with chicken. Serves 2-3.

Crunchy Chicken

1 cup corn bread stuffing mix

1 pound boneless, skinless chicken breasts

1 teaspoon vegetable oil

Heat oven to 350 degrees. Put the stuffing into a plastic bag. Thoroughly crush the stuffing by carefully rolling over it with a rolling pin or soup can. Pour 1 teaspoon vegetable oil in the center of a cookie sheet and spread it around the entire pan. Rinse chicken. Cut into small pieces. Drop several pieces of chicken in the bag, hold it closed, and shake it. Arrange chicken on pan, making sure pieces aren't touching. Bake for 15 minutes. Turn pieces over and bake 15 more minutes, or until coating is browned. Serves 4.

Variation: Serve with a dipping sauce created by combining 3 tablespoons honey and 3 tablespoons spicy brown mustard.

Baked Chicken in Sauce

1 pound skinless, boneless chicken breasts

½ cup of one of the following: Pace Picante sauce, Lea & Perrins White Wine Worcestershire Sauce, pizza sauce, honey mustard, or Italian dressing

Rinse and dry chicken.

Oven method: Preheat oven to 350 degrees. Spray a 9x7-inch pan with non-stick vegetable spray. Arrange chicken in pan. Put chicken into oven and bake uncovered for 20 minutes. Carefully spoon sauce over chicken. Return chicken to oven for an additional 10 minutes or until sauce is warm and chicken is done.

To microwave: Place chicken in a microwave-safe dish. Cover with plastic wrap, vent one corner. Cook on high 6-8 minutes. Rotate ¼ turn halfway through cooking time. Drain liquid. Spoon sauce over chicken. Cook for 1-2 minutes. Remove and serve. Serves 2-3.

Chicken in Gravy

4-6 skinless chicken pieces

1 1-ounce package chicken gravy mix

2 tablespoons flour

1 teaspoon crushed rosemary, optional

Note: You'll need 1 baking bag (found in grocer's plastic wrap section)

Rinse chicken and pat dry. Throw flour into baking bag and shake. (The flour prevents bag from bursting.) Pour into the bag gravy mix, rosemary, if using, and 1½ cups water. Squeeze bag to blend ingredients. Place bag into 13x9x2-inch baking pan. Sprinkle chicken with salt and pepper, if desired; place chicken in bag. Put tie wrap around open end of bag. Cut a small hole in middle of bag. Place pan in oven and bake at 350 degrees for 45-50 minutes. *Don't forget to make the cut in the bag.* Serves 4.

Variation: Add 4 sliced carrots and 2 sliced celery stalks to the bag.

Four-Star Chili Chicken

2 to 3 pound roasting chicken

1 28-ounce can Las Palmas green chili enchilada sauce

6-ounce package corn bread stuffing, optional

Preheat oven to 375 degrees. Rinse chicken. Remove fat and loosen skin around breast cavity. Baste with green chili sauce (under the skin, too). Place chicken in pan. At this point you can prepare packaged corn bread stuffing according to directions—which is mainly to add water, then fill chicken cavity with prepared stuffing. Pour remaining sauce over chicken. Bake for 1 to 1½ hours (depending upon size of chicken), baste occasionally. Serves 4.

Note: Put excess stuffing in a baking dish and bake for 30 minutes.

Lemonade Chicken Sauce

1 6-ounce can frozen lemonade

1/3 cup soy sauce

Combine ingredients. Rinse and dry 2 pounds chicken parts. Pour sauce over chicken. Barbecue or broil. Serves 4.

Variation: Add 1 clove minced garlic to the mixture.

Two-Lemon Chicken

3½ pound chicken

2 medium lemons

Preheat oven to 375 degrees. Line a 9x9x2-inch baking pan with aluminum foil. Set aside. Rinse and dry chicken with paper towels; sprinkle inside cavity with ½ teaspoon salt, if desired. Roll the lemons against a hard surface to loosen up the pulp. Prick lemons all over with a fork about 20 times and place inside chicken's cavity. Place chicken in pan; bake 1½ hours, or until chicken is white all the way through when you cut into it. Turn the chicken over halfway through baking time, if desired. Remove chicken from oven; let rest 10 minutes. Remove lemons from the chicken. As soon as they're cool enough to handle, halve and squeeze the lemons over the chicken. Serves 4-5.

Chicken Mediterranean

1 whole chicken

1 cup Italian dressing

Rinse chicken thoroughly; pat dry with paper towels. Poke holes all over chicken with a fork. Pour dressing over chicken. Marinade in refrigerator for 4 hours or overnight, turning occasionally. Remove chicken from marinade and bake in 350-degree oven for 55 minutes. Cover the chicken with foil for the first 40 minutes, and remove cover for the last 15 minutes for crispy, browned skin. Serves 4.

Chicken Mediterranean Lite

> **2-3 pounds chicken pieces, skin removed**
> **½ cup Italian dressing**

Rinse chicken and pat dry. In large baking dish, pour dressing over chicken. Prick chicken with a fork several times. Cover and marinate in refrigerator 4 hours or overnight, turning occasionally. Remove chicken from marinade. Bake at 350 degrees for 40 minutes, or until chicken is done. The chicken may also be grilled or broiled, turning and basting frequently with reserved marinade. Serves 3-4.

Moist Multi-Purpose Miracle Chicken

> **1 whole chicken**
> **¼ teaspoon garlic salt**

Rinse chicken and remove skin, if desired. Sprinkle garlic salt on chicken, place in a crockpot. Don't add water. Cover and cook on low for 7-8 hours. After cooking, you'll have delicious falling-off-the-bone chicken, making it the perfect way to prepare chicken for salads, fillings, casseroles—or by itself as an entree. The name says it all—the chicken even browns! Serves 4-5.

Variation: Add 1 squeeze of lemon or ¼ teaspoon rosemary.

Rosemary Chicken

> **2-3 pounds chicken parts**
> **2 teaspoons dried rosemary, divided use**
> **1/3 cup flour**

Rinse and dry chicken. Combine 1 teaspoon rosemary and flour in a shallow dish. Dredge chicken in the mixture. Coat a large baking pan with 1 teaspoon oil. Arrange chicken in pan; bake at 400 degrees without turning chicken, for 40 minutes. About 15 minutes before chicken is done, brush with pan drippings and sprinkle with remaining 1 teaspoon rosemary. Serves 4.

Saucy Italian Chicken

> **4 chicken breasts, skin removed**
> **1 14-ounce can or jar spaghetti sauce**
> **2 tablespoons flour**

Note: You'll need 1 baking bag (found in the plastic wrap section of the grocery store)

Rinse chicken, remove and discard skin, if desired. Throw flour into baking bag and shake. Add spaghetti sauce to the bag; squeeze the bag to blend in flour. (The flour prevents the bag from bursting.) Place chicken in bag. Put tie wrap around open end of bag; place bag into 13x9x2-inch baking pan. Cut a small hole in middle of bag. Place pan in oven and bake at 350 degrees for 35-40 minutes. *Don't forget to make the cut in the bag.* Serve the chicken and sauce over cooked pasta, if desired. Serves 4.

Variation: Add to bag 1 medium green pepper, coarsely chopped.

Savory Onion Chicken

> **1 chicken, cut-up, or 4 chicken breasts**
> **1 1.5-ounce package dry onion soup mix**
> **4 tablespoons butter, melted**

Rinse and dry chicken. Dip chicken pieces into melted butter, then roll in dry soup mix. Place chicken in a 12x8-inch microwave-safe dish. Cover with wax paper. Microwave on high for 18 to 20 minutes, turning halfway through heating time. Let stand for 5 minutes. Serves 4.

Variation: Throw several cloves of peeled garlic and/or a couple of sprigs of rosemary or tarragon in the bird, along with the lemons. When the chicken is done, so is the garlic.

Note: Olive oil or water may be substituted for the butter.

Spicy Baked Chicken Coating

> **1 1-ounce package Ranch party-dip mix**
> **½ cup instant mashed potato flakes**

Spray a baking pan with non-stick spray, or grease with shortening or butter. Combine Ranch mix with potato flakes in a flat dish. Rinse 1-2 pounds chicken parts, skin removed. Press chicken pieces into mix, one at a time. Place chicken in pan. Spray chicken lightly with non-stick spray. Bake at 400 degrees for 35-40 minutes. Serves 4.

Taco Chicken

> **2 pounds chicken pieces, skin removed**
> **1 1-ounce envelope taco seasoning**

Remove skin from chicken (if desired), rinse chicken, and pat dry.

Microwave method: Place chicken in a microwave-safe dish. Sprinkle both sides of chicken with taco seasoning. Cover with wax paper, cook on high for 8-12 minutes, giving the dish a ½ turn after 4 minutes. Let stand for 5 minutes, checking for absence of pinkness next to the bone.

Oven method: Spray a baking pan with non-stick vegetable spray. Prepare chicken as above. Bake for 40-50 minutes in a 350-degree oven. Serves 2-3.

Note: Try chicken wrapped in tortillas or served in a green salad.

Teriyaki Chicken—Crockpot Version

> **5 boneless, skinless chicken breasts**
> **¼ cup teriyaki sauce**

Rinse chicken, pat dry and place in a crockpot. Pour teriyaki sauce over the chicken, cover, and cook on low for 7-8 hours or until done. Serves 4-5.

Zippy Chicken

> **1 pound boneless, skinless chicken breasts, rinsed and sliced thin**
>
> **¼ cup Lea & Perrins White Wine Worcestershire sauce**
>
> **2 tablespoons butter**
>
> **¼ cup flour, optional**

Melt 2 tablespoons butter in a skillet over medium heat. Dredge chicken in ¼ cup flour, if desired. Sauté chicken until lightly browned on both sides, about 2-3 minutes per side; move chicken occasionally so that it doesn't weld to the skillet. Remove to a plate and keep warm. Pour in Worcestershire sauce and cook over medium heat, scraping the bottom of the skillet with a spatula until liquid is reduced to create a sauce, about 2 minutes. Pour sauce over chicken and serve. Serves 3-4.

Turkey Patties

> **1 pound ground turkey**
>
> **1 2-ounce envelope onion soup mix**

Mix turkey with soup mix. Shape into 4-6 patties. Spray a large skillet with non-stick vegetable spray. Brown patties over medium heat until cooked, about 4-5 minutes each side. Remove patties from heat. In the skillet, bring ½ cup hot water to boil, scraping up little bits from the bottom of the skillet to create a gravy. Serve gravy over patties. Serves 4. (They'll think it's beef.) Great with mashed potatoes!

Variation: Substitute ground beef for turkey. Grill or broil until done.

Roasted Barbecue Turkey Breast (for sandwiches)

1 2-pound turkey breast or roast

1 cup bottled barbecue sauce

Preheat oven to 350 degrees. Spray a baking dish with non-stick vegetable spray. Rinse and pat dry turkey breast; place in dish with skin side up. Add ¼ cup water. Cover turkey with foil. Bake 45 minutes, remove foil. Bake 45 minutes more, basting occasionally, if desired. Remove from oven and let stand 15 minutes. Refrigerate at least 1 hour. Shred turkey to make 2 cups. Combine shredded turkey and barbecue sauce in a medium saucepan. Heat and stir over medium heat for 5 minutes. Serve on toasted buns. Serves 4.

❧ Seafood ❧

Pesto Salmon

1 pound salmon steaks or filets

½ cup pesto

Preheat oven to 350 degrees. Spray baking dish with non-stick vegetable spray. Place 2 pieces of salmon in center of dish and cover each piece with half the pesto. Bake for 20 minutes or until done. Serves 2 impressively!

Hot Stuff Shrimp

1 pound gulf shrimp (12 to 15 shrimp), peeled and deveined

1 to 2 teaspoons Jamaican dry seasoning mix

2 tablespoons butter, optional

Peel and devein shrimp. Heat butter, if using, in a heavy skillet, or use non-stick vegetable spray. Cook shrimp for 5-6 minutes over medium heat. When shrimp is slightly browned, add Jamaican seasoning mix to taste. Serves 2-3.

Superb Shrimp

2 pounds gulf shrimp (25 to 30 shrimp), peeled

¼ cup unsalted butter

1 teaspoon tarragon vinegar, optional

Peel and devein shrimp. Place in a medium saucepan and cover with water, adding ½ teaspoon salt. Cook for 3 minutes over medium heat; remove from water after 3 minutes. Heat butter in a heavy skillet. When butter starts to bubble, add cooked shrimp. Stir slightly while sautéing. When shrimp is slightly browned, season with a few dashes of tarragon vinegar, if using, to add a subtle sweetness. Serves 6.

Fish in Sauce (chicken in sauce, without the feathers...)

1 pound fish fillets

½ cup of one of the following: Pace Picante sauce, Lea & Perrins White Wine Worcestershire Sauce, teriyaki sauce or French dressing

Oven method: Preheat oven to 450 degrees. Bake fish uncovered, for 4-7 minutes per ½ inch thickness. Drain liquid. Pour sauce over fish. Return to oven for 2 minutes.

Microwave method: Place fish in microwave-safe dish and cover with plastic wrap, vent one corner. Cook on high for 4-6 minutes. Rotate ¼ turn halfway through cooking. Drain liquid. Spoon sauce over fish. Cook for 1-2 minutes. Remove and serve. Serves 4.

Golden Coating for Fish

½ cup mayonnaise

½ cup bread crumbs

Dip 1 pound fish fillets, flounder or cod, in mayonnaise, then bread crumbs. Sprinkle with salt and pepper, if desired. Bake at 375 degrees for 15-20 minutes. Or cover with wax paper and microwave on high 5 to 8 minutes until fish flakes easily. Serves 4.

Tartar Fish

1 pound fish fillets, flounder, sole or cod

¾ cup bottled tartar sauce

Spoon sauce on each fish fillet. Broil until done. Or microwave on high 5 to 8 minutes until fish flakes easily. Serves 4.

Variation: Mix ¼ cup mayonnaise (reduced calorie mayonnaise, if desired) with 2 tablespoons fresh lemon juice, in place of tartar sauce.

8

Pasta Main Courses

Creamy Pasta Sauce

> 1 6-ounce container ricotta cheese
>
> ½ cup Parmesan cheese
>
> ¼ teaspoon nutmeg, optional

Prepare tubular pasta according to package directions. Mix ricotta cheese with enough pasta cooking water (a tablespoon or two) to create a sauce. Add grated Parmesan cheese and nutmeg, if desired, and toss. Serves 2-3.

Three-Ingredient Creamy Pasta Sauce

> 1 7-ounce jar roasted red peppers, drained
>
> 1 10-ounce can chicken broth
>
> 1 3-ounce package cream cheese

Mix red peppers and broth in a blender. Pour into a medium saucepan. Heat to simmering over medium-low heat; whisk in cream cheese. Pour over cooked pasta. Serves 2-3.

Hasty Herb & Garlic Pasta Sauce

> 1 4-ounce container Light Alouette garlic and herb spreadable cheese
>
> ¼ cup Parmesan cheese

Cook pasta according to package directions; drain. Immediately add 2 ounces or more of garlic and herb spreadable cheese. Top with Parmesan cheese. Serve hot or cold. Serves 4.

Speedy Stroganoff Sauce

> **1 10-ounce can cream of mushroom soup**
> **¼ cup plain yogurt, or sour cream**

Combine ingredients in small saucepan and heat over medium flame, stirring. Pour over cooked pasta. Serves 2-3.

Spinach Pasta

> **1 10-ounce package frozen creamed spinach**
> **2 tablespoons Parmesan cheese**

Microwave or boil spinach packet according to package directions. Toss with freshly cooked pasta. Top with Parmesan cheese. Serves 2.

Speedy Ziti Sauce

> **1 30-ounce Ragu chunky gardenstyle pasta sauce**
> **½ cup reduced-fat ricotta cheese**

Preheat oven to 350 degrees. Combine 1½ cups sauce and ricotta in blender. Blend until smooth, 1 to 2 minutes. Prepare 1 12-ounce package ziti pasta according to package directions; drain. Place pasta in 13x9x2-inch baking dish. Stir in ricotta mixture; top with remaining sauce from jar. Bake for 10 minutes. Serves 6.

Variation: Top with ¼ cup grated Parmesan cheese.

9

Vegetables and Side Dishes

Artichokes

6 artichokes

2 tablespoons apple cider vinegar

Rinse artichokes. Cut off stems and also cut off ½ inch from the top of the artichokes. Place artichokes in a crockpot. Pour 2 cups hot water over the artichokes, then vinegar. Cover and cook on low for 6-8 hours.

Variation: After cooling artichokes a bit, remove center leaves and bristles with tongs to create a well. Fill with 2 tablespoons Ranch dressing. Dip leaves into dressing as you eat. Mmmmm.

French Artichokes

4 medium-size artichokes

½ cup French dressing

Rinse artichokes; cut off ½ inch from the top of the artichokes. Cut off the stems so the artichokes can be set upright. Place artichokes in a large pot; add enough water so that it comes up to no more than 1½ inches from the bottom of the pan. Spread open leaves of each artichoke. Drizzle about 2 tablespoons of dressing over each artichoke. Bring water to boil over high heat. Lower heat, but continue to boil for 30 to 45 minutes, depending on the size of the artichokes. Serves 4.

Variation: Insert slivers of 1 garlic clove between leaves, if desired.

Asparagus and Parmesan Cheese

> **1 pound asparagus**
> **1 tablespoon grated Parmesan cheese**

Rinse asparagus and cut off the tough lower ends.

Stove-top method: Half-fill medium saucepan with water; bring to boil over high heat. Place asparagus in boiling water, reduce heat to medium and boil for 15-20 minutes, uncovered. Place asparagus on a serving dish and sprinkle with Parmesan cheese.

Microwave method: Place trimmed asparagus in a microwave-safe oblong dish, cover with plastic wrap, and turn back one corner of the wrap to vent.   Microwave on high 10-13 minutes, rotating dish halfway. Carefully remove asparagus from water. Place on serving dish and sprinkle with Parmesan cheese. Serves 3-4.

Variation: Sprinkle 1 or 2 tablespoons Worcestershire sauce over asparagus, then sprinkle with Parmesan cheese.

Buttered Green Beans

> **1 pound green beans**
> **1-2 tablespoons butter, cut into pieces**

Cut off bean tips, rinse, and cut beans into 2-inch sections.

Stove-top method: Fill a large pot 2/3 full with water; bring to a boil. Add beans to boiling water, return water to a boil and reduce heat, cooking for 6-7 minutes. Drain beans and add butter, tossing to coat beans.

Microwave method: Place ½ cup water and trimmed beans into a 1-quart microwave-safe covered dish. Cover and microwave on high for 16 minutes, stirring after 7 minutes. Drain beans and add butter, tossing to coat beans. Serves 3-4.

Quick Stewed Green Beans

1 14-ounce can green beans, drained

1 14-ounce can stewed tomatoes with onions and spices

Drain green beans. Pour green beans, with tomatoes and their juices, into a medium saucepan and heat over a medium flame until warm; or microwave in a microwave-safe dish on high for 2-3 minutes. Serves 4.

Puréed Broccoli

1 bunch broccoli

2 teaspoons butter

¼ teaspoon nutmeg, optional

Rinse and cut stems from broccoli. Separate broccoli into florets. Steam, microwave (on high 3-4 minutes), or boil broccoli in water (4-6 minutes), until tender. Drain and put broccoli into a blender along with the butter and ¼ teaspoon nutmeg, if desired. Purée until smooth. Serves 4.

Variations: Add 2 peeled, minced shallots to the blender. Add a squeeze or two of fresh lemon juice.

Broccoli Boosted with Garlic

1 bunch broccoli (about 1½ pounds)

3 to 4 cloves garlic, chopped

¼ cup olive oil

Remove stems from broccoli and chop remaining broccoli in chunks. Throw broccoli into a medium saucepan with boiling water and cook until just tender, about 4-6 minutes. Drain broccoli and water. In same medium saucepan, combine ¼ cup olive oil and chopped garlic. Cook over low heat 2-3 minutes, stirring often. Add broccoli and salt to taste, if desired. Turn broccoli several times to lightly coat with garlic mixture. Makes 2 to 4 servings.

Braised Cabbage

> **1 head of cabbage**
> **2 tablespoons oil**
> **1 teaspoon sugar**

Slice cabbage into ¼-inch thick strips. Heat oil in a large wok or skillet. Sauté cabbage over medium heat until limp, turning often, about 10 minutes. Sprinkle with sugar. Serves 4-6.

Variations: Add 1 teaspoon sesame oil, sesame seeds, or vinegar.

Steamed Cabbage

> **½ head of cabbage**
> **¼ teaspoon celery seed**

Slice cabbage into 2-inch wedges, sprinkle with celery seed, and steam for 15 minutes. Serves 4. (Steaming does not make cabbage bitter, as does boiling it too long.)

Quick Carrots

> **2 cups carrots, sliced into ½-inch thick rounds**
> **1 teaspoon butter**

In a saucepan, bring carrots, butter and ¼ cup water to a boil. Cover, reduce heat to low and simmer 5 minutes. Remove cover, increase heat to medium-high and shake pan for about 2 minutes. Serves 3.

Braised Celery

> **1 cup of celery, about 3 large ribs**
> **1 10-ounce can chicken broth**

Cut ribs into 1-inch pieces. Place in saucepan and cover with chicken broth. Simmer 10-14 minutes over medium low heat or until tender. Remove celery from broth and serve. Serves 2.

Easy Corn for Two

2-4 ears of corn, leaves removed

2 tablespoons cider vinegar

2 tablespoons sugar

Place ears of corn in a large pot and cover corn with cold water (don't add salt). Add vinegar and sugar. Cook over medium heat for 6 to 7 minutes. Leave corn in hot water until ready to serve. This gives any corn a subtle, sweet flavor. Serves 2-4.

Easy Corn for a Crowd

12 ears of corn, leaves removed

pinch of sugar (1/16 teaspoon)

Place corn in a large pot half full of water, add sugar. Heat until boiling. Cover, remove from heat and let stand 15 minutes.

Fried Corn

6 ears fresh corn, leaves removed

2 tablespoons butter

Break ears in half and cut corn from cobs. Melt butter in a large skillet. Cook over medium heat, stirring occasionally, 10 minutes or until corn is lightly browned. Serves 4-6.

Variations: Add 1 tablespoon heavy cream to mixture in skillet.

Oven Roasted Corn

4-6 ears of corn, leaves removed

1 tablespoon butter, melted

Brush corn with melted butter. Sprinkle with salt, if desired. Place corn in baking pan. Roast/bake at 400 degrees for about 20 minutes. Serves 4-6.

Corn and Thyme

> **4 ears of fresh corn, leaves removed**
>
> **1 tablespoon butter**
>
> **2-3 tablespoons fresh thyme leaves**

Break ears in half and cut kernels from ears of corn. Put butter in a medium saucepan and warm over medium heat. When butter is melted, add corn kernels and cook for 10 minutes. About halfway through the cooking, stir in the fresh thyme. Serves 2-3.

Sautéed Eggplant

> **1 medium peeled eggplant, cut crosswise in ½-inch slices**
>
> **1 tablespoon sugar**
>
> **3 tablespoons olive oil**

Heat oil in frying pan. Place slices in oil and sprinkle with sugar. Sauté, turning once or twice, until golden brown. Drain on absorbent paper. Makes 6 servings.

Roasted Garlic

> **1 head of garlic**
>
> **1 tablespoon olive oil**

Preheat oven to 350 degrees. Cut the top off the garlic head. Place the unpeeled head of garlic on a sheet of 8x8-inch foil; drizzle olive oil on top of garlic. Twist foil closed. Bake for 30 minutes. Let garlic cool for 5 minutes, then remove cloves from the head by squeezing them gently. Spread garlic cloves on slices of toasted French bread, or serve as a side dish. Serves 2.

Variations: Substitute 1 tablespoon butter for the olive oil. Add 1 tablespoon of brandy to the butter, if desired.

Savory Mushrooms

2 cups fresh mushrooms, thinly sliced

3 tablespoons Italian dressing

Rinse and slice mushrooms; dry with paper towels. Place in bowl and combine with Italian dressing. Let marinade in refrigerator for at least 4 hours; stir occasionally. Serves 3-4.

Roasted Onion

1 medium yellow onion

1 tablespoon butter, cut up

Preheat oven to 350 degrees. Cut the top and bottom off the onion; peel off the outer skin. Place the onion on a sheet of 8x8-inch foil; place pieces of butter on top of onion. Twist foil closed. Bake for 1 hour. The result is sweet, mild and very tender. Serves 2.

Variation: Substitute 1 tablespoon soy sauce for the butter.

Mom's Famous Peas

1 15-ounce can peas, undrained

1 8-ounce can tomato sauce

¼ teaspoon cumin

Place all ingredients into a medium saucepan. Heat over medium heat to boiling. For those people who like peas, these are legendary. Serves 4-6.

Cheesy Potatoes

4 medium baking potatoes

1 5-ounce package frozen broccoli in cheese sauce

Preheat oven to 400 degrees. Scrub potatoes under faucet, dry, prick several times with a fork and place in oven directly on rack. Bake at least 1 hour. Potatoes are fully cooked when you can stick a fork in the center and it feels soft. Just before serving, split each potato lengthwise and pour cheese sauce in the center of each. Garnish with chopped parsley, if desired. Serves 4.

Kids' Favorite Potatoes

2-4 medium baking potatoes

¼ teaspoon garlic salt

1 tablespoon olive oil

Preheat oven to 400 degrees. Scrub potatoes under faucet. Don't peel potatoes, but cut in half lengthwise. Sprinkle each cut half with garlic salt, and fresh ground pepper, if desired. Coat a baking dish with olive oil. Place potatoes cut-side down. Bake for 45 minutes. Serves 2-4.

Oven Fries

4 medium potatoes

1 tablespoon oil

Preheat oven to 475 degrees. Scrub potatoes under faucet. Don't peel potatoes, but cut into ½ inch strips. Soak strips in water for at least 15 minutes to remove excess starch, then drain and pat them completely dry. Place slices in big bowl or bag, along with the oil, and mix or shake well. Spray a baking/cookie sheet with a non-stick vegetable spray. Pour potatoes in a single layer and bake for 30 minutes, or until golden, turning potatoes every 10 minutes. Sprinkle with salt and/or pepper. Serves 4.

Easy Roasted Potatoes

2-3 pounds white or red new potatoes

3 tablespoons olive oil

¼ teaspoon garlic powder, optional

Spray a large baking pan with non-stick vegetable spray. Rinse and slice potatoes into quarters and place in pan. Dribble oil over potatoes and sprinkle with the garlic powder, if using. If desired, sprinkle with salt and pepper. Roast for 1 hour at 375 degrees. Serves 4-5.

Baked Potatoes

2 baking potatoes

4 tablespoons butter

2 to 4 ounces grated cheddar cheese, optional

An hour and fifteen minutes before you want to eat, preheat the oven to 400 degrees. Scrub and dry the potatoes, and pierce with a fork 4-5 times. (Rub potatoes with vegetable oil for crispy skins and to decrease baking time by 10 minutes.) Place the potatoes in the oven. After 1 hour and 15 minutes, remove the potatoes from the oven, split them open lengthwise, and top with butter. Season with salt and pepper, if desired. Serves 2.

Variations: After performing the above, slip in 1 ounce of grated cheddar cheese (or Alouette gourmet spreadable garlic and herb cheese) into each potato. Wrap the potatoes in foil and return to the oven for 10 minutes. Remove and serve.

Two-Ingredient Toppings for Plain Baked Potatoes

- **Butter and parsley**
- **Parmesan cheese and fresh ground pepper**
- **Salsa flavored Cheez Whiz (melted) and diced canned chiles**

Jamaican-Spiced Hot! Potatoes

> **2 baking potatoes**
>
> **¼ teaspoon Jamaican jerk spice**

Preheat oven to 400 degrees. Scrub and dry the potatoes, and pierce with fork 4-5 times. Put the potatoes in the oven. After 1 hour and 15 minutes, remove the potatoes from the oven and split them open lengthwise. Top each potato with ¼ teaspoon jerk spice and lightly combine with fork. Serves 2.

Basic Two-Ingredient Low-Cal Mashed Potatoes

> **6 medium potatoes**
>
> **1 10-ounce can chicken broth**

Scrub potatoes; remove skins before or after cooking. Cut potatoes into halves. Place potatoes in medium saucepan and cover with water. Bring to a boil over high heat, then turn down to medium heat and cook 25-30 minutes, covered. Drain and mash. Add ¾ cup chicken broth; mash until fluffy. Serves 6 to 8.

Ranch Potatoes

> **6 potatoes**
>
> **1 2-ounce package Hidden Valley Original Ranch Salad Dressing Mix (dry ingredients)**
>
> **¾ cup milk**
>
> **3 tablespoons butter or margarine, optional**

Scrub potatoes; remove skins before or after cooking. Cut potatoes into halves. Place potatoes in medium saucepan and cover with water. Bring to a boil over high heat, then turn down to medium heat and cook 25-30 minutes, covered. Drain water and mash potatoes. Add ¾ cup milk; mash until fluffy. (Instead of boiling, potatoes may also be microwaved.) . Stir in dry salad dressing mix. If desired, add 3 tablespoons butter or margarine. Serves 6 to 8.

Garlic-Herb Mashed Potatoes

1 pound red potatoes (peeled if desired), cut into 2-inch pieces

¼ cup garlic- and herb-flavored soft cheese such as Alouette or Boursin, (found in the dairy case next to other specialty cheese)

¼ cup milk, optional

Place rinsed and cut potatoes in large saucepan; cover with water. Simmer potatoes in water until tender, about 10 minutes. Drain potatoes and return to pan. Mash potatoes with soft cheese and, if desired, milk, salt and pepper, until they are smooth. Serves 2.

Low-Cal Gravy

½ cup peeled shallots, about 4 or 5 shallots

½ cup canned beef broth

¼ teaspoon olive oil, optional

Peel shallots and rub with oil, if using. Place shallots in a shallow baking pan and roast in a 375-degree oven for 30-40 minutes, or until they caramelize (areas turn brown). Remove from oven and purée with broth. Makes ¾ cup gravy.

Browned Sweet Potatoes

1 pound sweet potatoes (2 medium), grated

¼ teaspoon ground cumin

1 tablespoon olive oil

Peel and grate sweet potatoes, sprinkle with cumin. Heat oil in a medium skillet over medium-high flame. Add sweet potatoes and lightly flatten to cover skillet bottom. Brown on both sides, about 2 minutes per side. Serves 3-4.

Roasted Sweet Potato Slices

> **2 large sweet potatoes, or yams (about 3 pounds)**
>
> **2 tablespoons olive oil, divided use**

Heat oven to 350 degrees. Peel potatoes and cut into ¼-inch thick round slices. Apply 1 tablespoon oil to 2 baking sheets. Arrange potato slices in single layers and brush with remaining 1 tablespoon of oil. Sprinkle with salt and pepper, if desired. Bake 45-50 minutes, or until centers are tender and edges are brown. Serves 2-3.

Sweet Potato Topping

> **1 tablespoon sugar**
>
> **1 teaspoon cinnamon**
>
> **2 tablespoons olive oil, divided use**

Heat oven to 350 degrees. Peel 2 sweet potatoes or yams; cut into ¼-inch thick round slices. Apply 1 tablespoon oil to 2 baking sheets. Arrange potato slices in single layers and brush with remaining 1 tablespoon oil. Bake 45-50 minutes, or until centers are tender and edges are brown. Turn slices every 15 minutes during roasting. Combine the sugar and cinnamon; sprinkle it over the potatoes for the last 5 minutes of baking. Serves 4.

Sweet Potato Boats

> **2-4 sweet potatoes or yams**
>
> **6 miniature marshmallows, or 4 cut-up large marshmallows**

Scrub and dry potatoes. Prick potatoes with fork several times. Place potatoes in oven and bake for 1 hour at 375 degrees. After baking, cut cross in potato tops; push down on four cut corners. Insert marshmallows and return to oven for 5 minutes. Serves 2-4.

Two-Ingredient Toppings for Baked Sweet Potatoes or Yams

- 1 tablespoon butter and ½ teaspoon orange juice per potato
- 1 tablespoon butter and ½ tablespoon brown sugar per potato

Very Low-Cal Potato and Yam Purée

2 potatoes

2 yams

Scrub and dry potatoes; prick with a fork several times.

Oven method: Bake in oven for 1 hour at 400 degrees. Remove from oven; remove skins. Mash with potatoes and yams with a potato masher or fork.

Microwave method: Instead of baking or boiling, potatoes and yams may be microwaved on high for 12-14 minutes. Continue as above. Serves 4.

Brown Rice with Pine Nuts

1 cup uncooked brown rice

¼ cup toasted pine nuts

1 teaspoon salt, optional

Throw pine nuts into a medium saucepan on medium heat, shaking pan occasionally, for about 3 minutes until browned. Set aside pine nuts. In same saucepan, bring 2½ cups of water to boil with 1 teaspoon salt, if using. Add brown rice. Let water return to boiling, cover with a lid, and lower heat to simmer. Cook for 1 hour, without lifting lid or stirring rice (which makes rice gummy). After rice has cooked, stir in toasted pine nuts. Serves 4-6.

Curried Rice

1 cup instant rice

1 tablespoon curry powder

In a small heavy saucepan, bring 1 cup of water to boil. Add rice and curry powder; stir. Cover, reduce heat to low, and cook until liquid is evaporated and rice is tender, about 7 minutes. Makes 1 cup.

Green Rice or South-of-the-Border Rice

½ cup white rice

1 4-ounce can chopped mild green chiles

1 10-ounce can chicken broth, optional

In a small heavy saucepan, bring ¾ cup water, or chicken broth, if using, to boil. Add rice and chiles; stir. Cover, reduce heat to low, and cook until liquid is evaporated and rice is tender, about 20 minutes. Serves 2.

French Rice

1 10-ounce can onion soup

1 cup raw rice, any type

In a medium saucepan, blend soup with 1 cup of water. Stir in rice. Cover and cook over medium heat for 20-25 minutes. Serves 4.

Rice Flavored with Broth

1 cup fast-cooking or regular white rice

1 10-ounce can chicken broth

Combine rice with broth in a medium saucepan. Bring to a boil. Reduce heat to very low. Cover pan and cook until all liquid is absorbed and rice is tender, about 5 minutes for fast-cooking rice, 17 minutes for regular white rice. Season with salt and pepper, if desired. Serves 4.

REALLY Hot Rice

1 cup quick-cooking rice

¼ teaspoon jerk seasoning (Jamaican dry spice mix)

Combine rice and 1 cup of water in a microwave-save dish. Cover and microwave on high for 5 minutes. Stir in ¼ teaspoon jerk seasoning. Serves 4.

Variation: Substitute 1 10-ounce can chicken broth for the water.

Quick Mushroom Rice

1 10-ounce can cream of mushroom soup

2 cups fast-cooking rice

In a medium saucepan, combine soup and 1 ¼ cups water. Bring to a boil over high heat. Stir in rice; cover. Remove from heat and let stand 5-7 minutes. Serves 6.

Variations: Substitute cream of chicken, or broccoli cheese soup for cream of mushroom soup. Add 1 soup can water or milk, according to directions on soup can.

Sautéed Spinach and Nutmeg

1 bunch spinach (about ¾ pound)

¼ teaspoon nutmeg

1-2 tablespoons olive oil

Discard coarse stems of spinach. Wash spinach thoroughly and drain. In large skillet, heat olive oil over moderate heat, about 1 minute. Sprinkle nutmeg over bottom of skillet and immediately add spinach. Sauté spinach over medium heat, stirring until wilted, about 3 minutes. Serves 2.

Tip: Remember that sautéed spinach will shrink faster than the wicked witch in the Wizard of Oz, so you'll need plenty.

Grated Squash

2 yellow squash

2 pattypan or zucchini

Rinse, but do not peel, squash. Grate the vegetables by hand or in a food processor. Place in medium saucepan with ¼ cup water and bring to a boil over high heat, stirring. Reduce heat to medium-low and cook, stirring, 3 to 4 minutes. Season to taste with salt and pepper. Serves 2 to 3.

Variations: Add 1 tablespoon butter. Add 1 tablespoon grated Parmesan cheese.

Spaghetti Squash and Sauce

1 15-ounce can spaghetti sauce

1 spaghetti squash

Preheat oven to 375 degrees. Rinse squash. Pierce shell of squash with fork several times. Place in an 8-inch wide baking pan. Bake, uncovered, until shell gives when gently pressed, about 1 hour. Halfway through baking, turn squash over. Cut squash in half lengthwise; scoop out and discard seeds. With a fork, pull strands from shell halves onto a platter (it will come out like spaghetti). Heat spaghetti sauce in a small saucepan; serve over spaghetti squash. Serves 4.

Hot Tomatoes

1 8-ounce can whole tomatoes

¼ cup crumbled blue cheese

Drain whole tomatoes. Cut in half horizontally and place cut side up in an 8x8-inch dish. Sprinkle with blue cheese and broil 4-5 minutes, or bake at 375 degrees for 10 minutes. Serves 4-6.

Variation: Substitute grated Parmesan cheese for blue cheese.

Tomato Aspic

1 3-ounce box lime Jell-O mix

1 15-ounce can stewed tomatoes, undrained

Heat 1 cup of water to boiling. Place Jell-O in a medium bowl. Pour boiling water over Jell-O, stirring constantly to dissolve. Stir in tomatoes with their juice. Refrigerate several hours before slicing/serving. Serves 6-8.

Roasted Vegetables

1 pound of vegetables, such as potatoes, carrots, eggplant, red or green peppers, celery, parsnips, turnips and/or zucchini

1 teaspoon olive oil

Preheat oven to 400 degrees. Scrub and dry vegetables. Rub or toss vegetables with oil. Prick potatoes with fork several times. Place in roasting pan. Sprinkle with salt and pepper, if desired. Turn vegetables occasionally while roasting, or just shake the pan. Roast for 1 hour. Serves 2-3.

Variation: Sprinkle vegetables with 1-2 teaspoons crushed rosemary.

Note: Roasting vegetables concentrates their flavor and brings out their natural sweetness. Pre-roasted vegetables are great to keep on hand in the refrigerator; just warm to eat. They're great as appetizers, in sandwiches, as toppings on a pizza, puréed with chicken broth for soup, or with eggs for breakfast.

Herbed Roasted Vegetables

> 1½ pounds assorted fresh vegetables, such as potatoes, squash, red or green peppers, celery, mushrooms, parsnips, turnips, carrots or zucchini
>
> 1 2-ounce envelope Lipton Recipe Secrets Savory Herb with Garlic or Recipe Secrets Onion Soup mix
>
> 2 tablespoons olive or vegetable oil

Preheat oven to 450 degrees. Rinse and dry vegetables; cut into uniform 2-inch pieces. In a bowl, toss all ingredients until vegetables are coated. Spray a 13x9-inch baking or roasting pan with a non-stick vegetable coating. Spread vegetables into pan in one layer. Bake 25 minutes or until vegetables are tender, stirring once. Makes 4 servings.

Vegetable Custard Bake — 3-Ingredient

> 1 10-ounce package frozen chopped broccoli, thawed
>
> ½ pint heavy cream
>
> 1 cup shredded Parmesan cheese

Thaw broccoli, or place the opened package on a microwave-safe plate and microwave for 6 minutes on high. Drain excess liquid from broccoli. Preheat oven to 350 degrees. Place broccoli in the bottom of an ungreased 13x9-inch pan. Pour heavy cream over broccoli, then toss Parmesan cheese over both. Tamp down lightly with a spoon. Bake in oven for 30 minutes. So delicious, even non-broccoli fans love this dish. Serves 6.

Variation: Substitute 3-4 medium fresh zucchini for the broccoli. Slice unpeeled zucchini into ½-inch thick rounds and place in the pan.

10

Desserts

ಢ Chocolate and Other Decadent Desserts ఆ

Apricot Chocolate Drops

1 12-ounce package milk chocolate chips

½ cup dried apricots, chopped

½ cup unsalted peanuts, optional

Melt chocolate in a small saucepan over low heat, stirring often. Stir in apricots, and peanuts, if using. Drop teaspoonfuls on a waxed-paper-lined cookie sheet. Let stand in a cool place about 1 hour, until firm. Store in refrigerator. Makes 24 candies.

Creamed Brownies

2 brownies, store-purchased

1 pint vanilla ice cream

Place 2 brownies in 2 goblets; top with ice cream. Serves 2.

Chocolate Candied Ginger

¼ cup crystallized ginger, cut into dippable chunks

6 ounces milk chocolate chips

Melt chocolate in a small saucepan over low heat, stirring constantly until smooth. Remove from heat. Dip ginger pieces into chocolate one piece at a time to coat completely. Arrange on waxed paper. Let stand in a cool place until firm, about 1 hour. Store in refrigerator. This a very exotic flavor; not for the timid. Makes about 12 pieces.

Chocolate-Dipped Fruit

> **3 1-ounce squares semisweet chocolate (or 3 ounces milk chocolate chips)**
>
> **2 cups fresh fruit, such as strawberries, oranges, tangerines, bananas**

Stovetop method: Melt chocolate in a small saucepan over low heat, stirring constantly until smooth. Remove from heat.

Microwave method: Microwave chocolate in bowl on medium-high for 2 minutes, stirring after 1 minute. Stir until completely melted. Dip fruit sections one at a time into melted chocolate to coat halfway. Arrange on a cookie sheet lined with waxed paper. Let stand in a cool place until firm, about 1 hour. Store in refrigerator.

Variation: Substitute 3 1-ounce squares Baker's white chocolate. Instead of fruit, dip cookies or pretzels into chocolate.

Chocolate Nut Bark

> **1 12-ounce bag semi-sweet or milk chocolate chips**
>
> **¾ cup pecans, almonds or walnuts; shelled and toasted**

Toast nuts by placing them on a cookie sheet and baking them for 15 minutes in a 350 degree oven, or place nuts in a skillet or medium saucepan and heat over medium heat for about 10 minutes, stirring or shaking pan often. Melt chocolate in a saucepan over very low heat, stirring constantly until smooth. (Note: If you are using the same skillet or saucepan for both procedures, let it cool before adding chocolate, or you'll risk scorching the chocolate.) Remove saucepan from heat and stir in nuts. Pour onto waxed-paper-lined cookie sheet. Flatten with spatula so nuts are in a single layer. Let stand in a cool place for 1 hour. Refrigerate 1 hour until firm. Break or cut into 3-inch chunks. Makes about 9 pieces.

Chocolate Stack Cookies

> 1 4-ounce milk chocolate bar, or ½ cup milk chocolate chips
>
> 1½ cups corn flakes

Melt chocolate carefully in a microwave oven, or saucepan over low heat, stirring to prevent scorching. Slowly add corn flakes until mixture is thick and flakes are covered with chocolate. Drop by spoonfuls onto waxed paper. It's going to be difficult to restrain yourself, but let the stacks cool for 1 hour; cooling really changes the flavor. Makes 1 dozen.

Chocolate Turbans

> 1 sheet Pepperidge Farm Frozen Puff Pastry (this stuff is *easy* to use)
>
> 1 6-ounce package milk chocolate chips
>
> ¼ cup chopped walnuts, almonds or pecans, optional

Thaw pastry 30 minutes. Preheat oven to 450 degrees. On a lightly floured surface, roll pastry into a 12-inch square; cut into four 6-inch squares. In the center of each square, place ¼ cup chocolate chips and 1 tablespoon chopped nuts, if desired. Bring pastry corners together just above chocolate. In one hand, grasp corners and twist as if twisting a lid onto a jar. Fan out corners. Place on ungreased baking sheet. Bake 10-15 minutes or until golden brown. Let stand at least 10 minutes. These are pretty tasty at room temperature, too. Serves 4.

Variation: After baking, sprinkle with powdered sugar, if desired.

Fast-Fix Chocolate Frosting

> **12 ounces semisweet or milk chocolate chips**
>
> **2 cups (1 pint) sour cream, room temperature**

Melt chocolate in microwave oven or double boiler on very low heat. Stir until smooth. Remove from heat; blend in sour cream. Spread this addictive frosting on pound cake or graham crackers. Makes 2 ½ cups.

Note: Unless sour cream is at room temperature, you'll end up with fudge instead of frosting... not the worst tragedy in the world!

Shiny Chocolate Glaze

> **1 6-ounce package semisweet chocolate chips**
>
> **1/3 cup heavy cream**

Melt chocolate in small saucepan over low heat. Stir in cream until well blended. Makes a great glaze for cake or a decadent sauce over ice cream. Makes about 1 cup.

Chocolate Mint Sauce

> **20 thin dark-chocolate-covered mints (from a 4 ounce package)**
>
> **1/3 cup heavy cream**

Combine ingredients in a small saucepan; heat over low flame. Stir constantly, about 3 minutes, until mints are melted. Let cool 10 minutes. Spoon over drained canned pear halves, apricots or mandarin orange segments. Serves 2.

Crunchy Chocolate Ice Cream Sundae

1 pint chocolate ice cream or frozen yogurt

1 4-ounce nut brittle candy bar, such as Skor or Heath bars

Hit unwrapped nut brittle bar with a hammer or heavy object several times to break candy into small pieces. Scoop ice cream into serving dishes; top with crushed nut brittle. Serves 4.

The Most Incredible Chocolate Pudding and/or Dipping Sauce

6 ounces milk chocolate chips

1/3 cup heavy/whipping cream

Combine chocolate and cream in medium saucepan; melt and stir over medium-low heat until smooth. Remove from heat. (At this point, you may stir in ½ teaspoon pure vanilla extract, ½ teaspoon almond extract, or 1 tablespoon brandy or liqueur, if desired.) For a pudding, refrigerate at least 2-3 hours or overnight. (This pudding is so deliciously rich that you should plan to serve it alongside a treadmill or rowing machine!) As a dipping sauce, immediately serve while still warm with whole strawberries, chunks of fruit and/or cake to dip into the chocolate. Makes 1/2 cup.

❧ Cookies and No-Bake Pie Crusts ❧

No-Bake Fig Newton Pie Crust

12 fig newtons

2 tablespoons butter, melted

Place fig newtons in a blender; whirl to make fine crumbs. Place crumbs in a 9-inch pie plate. Melt butter and pour over crumbs. Mix with a spoon until well combined; press mixture on bottom and sides of pie plate to form crust. Makes 1 pie crust ready for a no-bake or freezable filling.

Three-Ingredient (so shoot me—they're worth it!) Peanut Butter Cookies

> 1½ cups chunky peanut butter
>
> 1 cup sugar
>
> 2 unbeaten egg whites

Preheat oven to 375 degrees. Combine peanut butter and sugar. Add egg whites and blend. Roll into walnut-sized balls and place on ungreased cookie sheet. Flatten with a fork. Bake for 10-12 minutes. Makes 1 dozen.

❧ Dessert Cakes ❧

Simple 2-Ingredient Sauces, Toppings and Frostings

Serve these easy sauces over store-bought pound cake, angel food cake, or any plain cake. When mixing ingredients, use a small bowl and don't measure them over the bowl—you may end up with ½ cup of an ingredient instead of ½ teaspoon!

- ¼ cup orange juice and 1 cup powdered sugar. Mix and let sit for 5 minutes to let sugar dissolve. (Especially good served over slices of chocolate swirl pound cake.)

- 1 6-ounce container pina colada yogurt and 2 tablespoons vodka. Mix and refrigerate until serving. Serve over individual cake slices.

- 2 4-ounce snack-size containers vanilla pudding and ½ cup chocolate sauce. Spread pudding between cake slices; top with chocolate sauce. Very chocolate eclair-like.

Easy Fresh Fruit Cake Filling

1½ cups fresh fruit, such as raspberries, peaches, nectarines or strawberries

1 cup ricotta cheese (found in the dairy case with other packaged cream cheese, etc.)

1 purchased sponge or pound cake

Rinse and cut the fruit; purée with the ricotta cheese. Cut the cake into 3 horizontal layers. Spread the mixture between the layers, stacking the layers as you proceed. Spread the remaining mixture on the top of the cake and on the sides. Serves 6-8.

Low-Fat Pound Cake 'Sandwich' Filling

1 8-ounce can pear halves

1 8-ounce container low-fat lemon yogurt

1 fat-free pound cake (purchased from the grocer)

Thinly slice pound cake horizontally. Drain pear halves; slice thinly. Spread yogurt on one cake half. Layer pear slices on top of yogurt. Top with remaining cake layer. Serves 8-10.

Strawberry Jell-O Cake Filling

1 6-ounce box raspberry Jell-O

2 10-ounce containers frozen sliced strawberries, partially thawed

1 10-inch angel food cake (purchased at the grocer's)

Pour Jell-O into a large bowl. Add 2 cups boiling water and stir until dissolved, about 2 minutes. Stir in partially thawed strawberries. Pour into a large Tupperware bowl. Throw the whole cake on top of the strawberry/raspberry Jell-O mixture. Top with a plate and refrigerate 2 hours. Unmold onto a plate. Serves 6-8.

Strawberry Filling for Angel Food Cake

>   **2-3 cups fresh strawberries, rinsed and sliced, divided use**
>
>   **1 12-ounce container frozen dessert topping, thawed**
>
>   **1 angel food cake, purchased**

Slice cake into 3 horizontal layers. Frost each layer with dessert topping and top with sliced strawberries, stacking each layer as you go. Garnish with sliced strawberries. Serves 6-8.

❧ Frozen Desserts ❧

Banana Ice Cream or Easy Dieter's Ice Cream

>   **4 ripe bananas, peeled**
>
>   **½ cup frozen berries, or other fruit for garnish**

Peel and slice the bananas; place them in a tightly sealed plastic bag in your freezer. Once frozen, whirl them in a blender on high speed until smooth. Spoon frozen purée into sherbet glasses and serve. For added flavor, top with frozen berries or fruit. Serves 2.

Berry Pie No-Bake Filling

>   **1 pint vanilla ice cream, softened, or vanilla yogurt**
>
>   **1 basket strawberries, or other berries hulled and rinsed**
>
>   **1 graham cracker crumb crust pie shell (found in the baking section at the grocery store)**

Slice strawberries, if using. In a large bowl, stir fruit into softened ice cream or yogurt. Pour into a ready-to-fill graham cracker pie shell. Cover and freeze at least 4 hours until firm. If pie is frozen overnight, let thaw 15-20 minutes before serving. Serves 6-8.

Tip: Soften ice cream by microwaving it on medium-low or defrost for 15 to 20 seconds for a pint, 45 seconds for a half-gallon. Let stand for 3 minutes before serving.

Berry Frozen

1 10-ounce package frozen raspberries, thawed

2 pints vanilla ice cream or yogurt

Blend berries in a blender until puréed. Strain purée; taste; add sugar if needed. Scoop ice cream or yogurt into 8 serving dishes. Spoon purée over scoops. Serves 8.

Frozen Dessert

1 angel food cake from the grocery store

1 pint frozen yogurt, your favorite flavor, softened

Slice the cake horizontally into 3 layers. Spread softened frozen yogurt between the layers. Wrap with foil or plastic wrap; freeze at least 2 hours before serving. Serves 6-8.

Frozen Fruit Ice

1 16-ounce package frozen strawberries, peaches or raspberries (thawed for 2 hours)

2 teaspoons honey

Remove frozen fruit from freezer 2 hours before serving. When ready to serve, put ¼ of the fruit in a blender or food processor; add honey to taste. Continue adding fruit until it is a thick purée. (Strawberry fruit ice is especially good over vanilla ice cream or pound cake.) Serves 3 or 4.

Fruit Sorbet

2 cups fruit, cut into chunks

¼ teaspoon vanilla or almond extract

Place fruit chunks into air-tight containers or sealed bags to freeze. Before serving, let frozen fruit thaw 30 minutes, then purée with extract in a blender or food processor. For a make-ahead dessert, just spoon purée directly into dessert dishes (or freezer container) and re-freeze until ready to serve. Serves 2.

Note: This is a great way to use overripe or leftover fruit.

Ice Cream Sandwiches

8 chocolate chip cookies (purchased, or homebaked using refrigerated cookie dough)

1 cup softened vanilla ice cream

Spread slightly softened ice cream between pairs of cookies to make sandwiches; freeze uncovered until firm (at least 1 hour). Wrap and freeze sandwiches at least 1 hour until ready to serve. Serves 4.

Variation: Use brownies in place of cookies.

Mississippi Mud Pie

1 prepared chocolate-flavored wafer pie shell (found in the frozen foods section)

1 quart (2 pints) softened chocolate-almond ice cream

½ cup purchased chocolate fudge sauce, optional

Fill pie shell with softened ice cream. (Stir softened ice cream in a mixing bowl until smooth, if necessary.) If desired, drizzle with chocolate sauce. Store in freezer at least several hours, until hard, before serving. Serves 8.

No-Bake Pumpkin Pie Filling

> 1 pint vanilla ice cream, softened
> 1 cup canned pumpkin pie filling with spices
> 1 graham cracker crumb crust shell

In a large bowl, stir pumpkin pie filling into softened vanilla ice cream. Pour into a ready-to-fill graham cracker crumb crust and freeze until firm, about 2 hours. If pie is frozen overnight, let thaw 15-20 minutes before serving. Serves 6-8.

Sherbet Splendor

> 1 pint fruit sherbet
> ¼ cup orange juice or wine, red or white

For each serving, generously fill a dessert glass with sherbet. Spoon over 1 tablespoon orange juice, or 2 tablespoons dry white or red wine. Garnish with fresh fruit, if desired. Serves 4.

Other Sherbet Combinations

- **Pineapple sherbet with orange juice.**
- **Lime sherbet with lemon juice and champagne.**
- **Lemon sherbet splashed with tequila.**

Snow Balls

> 1 pint of your favorite ice cream or frozen yogurt
> ½ cup shredded or canned coconut

Roll scoops of ice cream or yogurt in coconut. Wrap individually in aluminum foil and freeze until needed. Makes 4-5.

Variation: At serving time, top each snowball with a tablespoon of purchased chocolate syrup or canned cherry pie filling.

❧ Fruit Desserts ❧

Berry Shortcake

> **1 11-ounce package refrigerator biscuits**
>
> **2 cups fresh strawberries**
>
> **1 teaspoon sugar, optional**

Bake biscuits according to package directions. Split and set tops aside. Rinse and slice strawberries. Sprinkle with sugar, if desired. Divide half of strawberries evenly over biscuit bottoms. Replace tops. Top with remaining strawberry mixture. Serves 4.

Exotic Blueberries and Ginger

> **1 basket of fresh blueberries**
>
> **1½ tablespoons crystallized ginger, chopped**

Rinse blueberries, discarding mushy berries. Place berries in individual goblets and top with ginger. Serves 4.

Cantaloupe and Raspberries

> **1 ripe cantaloupe**
>
> **1 basket of raspberries**

Slice cantaloupe in half, remove seeds, and fill each half with raspberries. Serves 2.

Glistening Oranges in Grand Marnier

> **2 oranges**
>
> **2 tablespoons Grand Marnier**

Remove skin and membrane from oranges. Separate into sections. Place on 2 dessert plates and sprinkle each orange with 1 tablespoon each Grand Marnier. Serves 2.

Cloud Covering for Grapes

> **1 8-ounce container vanilla yogurt or sour cream**
>
> **¼ cup brown sugar**
>
> **¼ cup toasted pine nuts, optional**

Rinse 1 pound of seedless red flame grapes. Remove grapes from stems and place in individual serving dishes. Sprinkle grapes with toasted pine nuts, if using (see note). Spoon yogurt or sour cream over grapes; sprinkle with brown sugar. Put in refrigerator for at least ½ hour for sugar to 'melt'. Serves 4.

Note: Toast pine nuts by placing in a medium saucepan for 4-5 minutes over medium heat, stirring pan occasionally.

Papaya Heaven

> **1 ripe papaya**
>
> **2 scoops raspberry sherbet or frozen yogurt**

Cut papaya in half along its length and remove seeds. Top each papaya half with a scoop of sherbet. Serves 2.

Strawberries in Champagne

> **1 basket of fresh strawberries (or raspberries)**
>
> **1 small bottle of champagne**

Remove stems from rinsed strawberries. Place strawberries in stemmed champagne glasses and top with champagne. Serves 4.

Strawberry Creme

> **1 8-ounce container vanilla yogurt or sour cream**
>
> **¼ cup brown sugar**

Rinse 1 basket of strawberries. Dip strawberries into yogurt or sour cream, then into brown sugar. Serves 2-4.

෨ Sauces and Dessert Toppings ෨

Brandied Apple Topping

>1 15-ounce can apple pie filling
>¼ teaspoon allspice
>1 tablespoon brandy, optional

In medium saucepan, heat apple pie filling with allspice, and brandy, if desired. Cook over medium-high heat 3-4 minutes until heated through. Top individual scoops of vanilla ice cream with topping. Serves 4 to 6.

'Cots n' Cream Topping

>1 4-ounce can pitted apricots or apricot halves
>1 tablespoon orange juice

Purée apricots, their syrup and orange juice in blender. Place in saucepan and bring to boil Let boil over medium-high heat 5 to 6 minutes, stirring once. Remove from heat. Serve over vanilla ice cream or pound cake. Serves 4.

Quick Caramel Sauce

>2/3 cup heavy cream
>10 individual caramel candies

Combine cream and caramels in a small saucepan. Cook over medium-low heat, stirring constantly, 5 to 6 minutes, until caramel melts and mixture comes to a gentle boil. Serve over vanilla ice cream. This is also an excellent dipping sauce for apple wedges, or served as a topping over warm apple pie. Serves 3-4.

Variation: Top sauce with chopped pecans.

Cherry Sauce

1 15-ounce can cherry pie filling (may substitute 1 cup washed and pitted fresh cherries)

½ teaspoon sugar, optional

Whirl cherries, and sugar, if using, in a blender until smooth (omit sugar for a tart flavor). Pour over ice cream, pound cake or fresh fruit. Makes 1 cup sauce.

Heath Heaven

2 Heath Bars

1 pint vanilla ice cream

Freeze 2 Heath Bars. Leave frozen bars wrapped and hit with a hammer 10 times. Sprinkle Heath dust over scoops of ice cream. Wow! Serves 4.

11

Beverages

Banana Daiquiri

> **1 cup orange juice, chilled**
> **1 medium banana, ripe**
> **¾ cup cracked ice**

In a blender combine orange juice, banana and ice. Process until frothy. Serves 2.

Variation: Substitute pineapple juice for the orange juice.

Berry-Berry Smoothie

> **1 pint raspberry sherbet or frozen raspberry yogurt**
> **2 cups cold milk (non-fat milk works just as well)**

Blend ingredients for 15 seconds on high speed. Serves 2.

Variation: Substitute chilled cranberry juice cocktail for milk.

Low-Cal Cantaloupe Crush

> **1 cantaloupe, chilled and cubed**
> **1 8-ounce container plain low-fat yogurt**

In a blender or food processor, process cantaloupe, yogurt and ½ cup cracked ice until smooth. Serves 4.

Variations: Add ¼ cup orange juice to blend. Substitute fresh peaches, mango or honeydew melon for the cantaloupe.

Champagne Burst

> 1 part champagne, chilled
>
> 1 part orange juice, chilled

Pour equal parts champagne and orange juice into a stemmed glass.

Variation: Add ½ teaspoon grenadine per glass.

Champagne Cocktail

> 8 ounces champagne, chilled
>
> 1 sugar cube saturated with Angostura aromatic bitters (found where cocktail mixes are shelved)

Drop an Angostura-saturated (4-5 splashes) sugar cube into a stemmed glass and fill with chilled champagne.

Cranberry-Raspberry Sling

> 2 cups low-calorie cranberry juice cocktail, chilled
>
> 1 cup fresh or frozen raspberries, thawed

Blend ingredients on high speed until almost smooth. Sieve mixture; discard seeds. Return to blender.   Add 1 cup ice cubes. Blend until smooth. Serves 4.

Citrus Cream

> 1 cup orange juice
>
> 1 cup lemon sherbet

Combine orange juice and lemon sherbet in a blender, whirl for 1 minute. Serves 2.

Variation: Substitute orange sherbet for lemon sherbet.

50/50 Peach Smoothie

> 1 cup apple juice, chilled
>
> 1 8-ounce can peaches, chilled and drained, or fresh peaches

In a blender, purée apple juice and peaches. Serves 2.

Variation: Top with a scoop of frozen raspberry yogurt!

Make-Ahead Frosty Shake

> 1 8-ounce container non-fat strawberry yogurt
>
> 1 8-ounce (snack size) container cranberry juice cocktail, chilled

Scoop yogurt into a plastic container with a tight-fitting lid; add cranberry juice. Shake briefly, and seal shut with lid. Freeze at least 4 hours or up to 1 month. Perfect for packing in a lunch. Will thaw in 4 to 5 hours. Serves 1.

Frozen Yogurt Float

> 1 pint frozen vanilla or raspberry yogurt
>
> 1 10-ounce can club soda, chilled
>
> sprinkle of nutmeg, optional

Scoop yogurt into 2 tall glasses. Fill with club soda. Sprinkle with nutmeg, if desired. Serves 2.

Low-Cal Sipper

> 4 12-ounce cans or 6 cups diet cola, chilled
>
> 1 tablespoon powdered low-cal lemon drink mix

Pour soda into large pitcher. Stir in lemon-drink mix. Divide among 4 large glasses filled with ice. Cola with a twist! Serves 4.

Low-Cal Float

> 4 12-ounce cans or 6 cups diet cola, root beer or
> lemon-flavored soda, chilled
>
> 2 cups frozen yogurt, any flavor

Divide soda among 4 large glasses. Top with scoops of your favorite frozen yogurt. Serves 4.

Sparkling Lemonade

> 2 25-ounce bottles Perrier, or other carbonated water
>
> 1 6-ounce container frozen Minute Maid lemonade,
> partially thawed
>
> 2 tablespoons mint leaves, optional

Mix Perrier with lemonade, and mint, if using. Serves 8.

Frozen Strawberry Daiquiris

> 1 6-ounce can frozen limeade, partially thawed
>
> 1 basket fresh strawberries, or 1 10-ounce container
> frozen strawberries, partially thawed
>
> 6 ounces white rum, optional

In a blender, combine the limeade, strawberries, and rum, if using. Add 3 cups cracked ice and blend until slushy, about 45 seconds. Makes 4 servings.

Variations: Add 1 tablespoon sugar. Add 2 teaspoons grenadine (a syrup found shelved with the cocktail mixes at the grocer's).

Note: If using alcohol, the mixture can be prepared ahead of time. Just pop a pitcher of daiquiris in the freezer; the alcohol in the rum will keep the mixture slushy. The daiquiris are equally delicious without the rum.

Strawberry-Orange Juice

3 ounces frozen whole strawberries

5 ounces orange juice

1 tablespoon vodka, optional

Combine ingredients in a blender. Add 1 ounce vodka, if desired. Serves 1.

Sunset Sip

3 cups fresh raspberries

¾ cup frozen limeade concentrate

Place raspberries, limeade and 1 cup cracked ice in a blender. Process until smooth. Serves 4.

Variation: Add 2 12-ounce cans 7-Up *after* blending.

Tropical Blend

1 15-ounce Dole Tropical Fruit Salad (chill can in refrigerator)

1 8-ounce container low-fat vanilla yogurt

Combine undrained tropical fruit salad and yogurt in blender. Purée 1 minute.   Serves 2.

Variation: After blending, stir in 1 12-ounce can lemon-lime soda. Serves 4.

Island Smoothie

8 ounces coconut milk, chilled

1 ripe banana

Combine coconut milk and peeled banana in a blender. Serves 1.

Two-Ingredient Beverage Combinations

Just add ice cubes...

- ½ cup fruit juice and 1 cup soda (lemon lime, Sprite, Fresca, etc.)

- ½ cup wine (any color) and 1 cup soda (tonic water, Sprite, lemon lime or club soda)

- 3 cups orange juice and 1½ cups club soda

- Equal parts chilled ginger ale and chilled pineapple juice

- Equal parts chilled ginger ale and iced tea

- ¾ cup unsweetened pink grapefruit juice and 1 tablespoon grenadine (found with the cocktail mixes at the grocer's)

- 1 glass orange juice and 1 tablespoon grenadine. (The combination creates a lovely sunrise effect, stir before sipping.)

Index